PREPARING *My* HEART FOR

GRANDPARENTING

PREPARING MY HEART FOR

GRANDPARENTING

AMG
Publishers

LYDIA E. HARRIS

Preparing My Heart for Grandparenting:
For Grandparents at Any Stage of the Journey

Copyright © 2010 by Lydia E. Harris
Published by AMG Publishers, Inc.
6815 Shallowford Rd.
Chattanooga, Tennessee 37421

ISBN 13: 978-0-89957013-6
ISBN 10: 0-89957-013-5
First Printing—September 2010

Cover designed by Daryle Beam at BrightBoy Design, Chattanooga, TN
Interior design and typesetting by Kristin Goble at PerfecType, Nashville, TN
Edited and proofread by Rich Cairnes and Rick Steele
Back cover photo courtesy of Jonathan M. Harris

Printed in Canada
15 14 13 12 11 10 –T– 7 6 5 4 3 2 1

Dedicated with love to my husband, Milt,
a devoted father and
praying grandfather,
and to our precious grandchildren.

Acknowledgments

This Bible study is a gift of love to you from many people.

Thanks to my family and friends who encouraged me, prayed throughout the project, and even prepared meals so I had more time to write!

Special thanks to my prayer team: Nancy Aguilar, Margaret Been, Barbara Bryden, Jeanetta Chrystie, Bill and Erna Craven, Ramona Davis, Cheryl Faull, Dianna Ferguson, Glenn and Helen Garner, Lori Nienau, Joan McClenny, and Colleen Reph. Thanks also to others who prayed. What a gift!

I'm also grateful to the dozens of grandparents who completed grandparenting surveys and shared stories and insights. Your wisdom helped shape the study. For testing the Bible study, thanks go to Ruth Roetcisoender and her GRAND ladies and other grandparents who gave input.

I also value the help of fellow writers and editors: Nancy Aguilar, Barbara Bryden, Delora Buoy, Jeanetta Chrystie, Agnes Lawless Elkins, Mary Hake, Barbara Koshar, Barbara Henry Proctor, Gail Welborn, and others.

Thanks also to my church family at Northshore Baptist Church in Bothell, Washington, for their encouragement and prayers. I am grateful for many years of solid Bible teaching from Pastor Jan David Hettinga, Pastor Jonathan Alexander, and others.

I'm deeply grateful to Ann Marie Stewart, my niece and writer of three Bible studies in the "Preparing My Heart" series. Ann, your encouragement and mentoring kept me going, and your editing was invaluable. You're a blessing.

Of course, thanks to my children and grandchildren for their support. Without them I wouldn't have written on the subject of grandparenting. Thank you, Steve and Anita Faull and grandchildren Peter and Alex. And thanks also to Jonathan and Amy Harris and grandchildren Clara, Owen, and Anna Joy. I love you all.

Much love goes to my husband, Milt Harris, who prayed, encouraged, critiqued my writing, picked up the slack at home, and served as the president of my fan club. I'd marry you again, Sweetie.

Finally, thanks to AMG Publishers for publishing this book, to the late Dan Penwell for encouraging me to write, and to Rick Steele and Rich Cairnes for editing this study.

To God be the glory!

About the Author

LYDIA E. HARRIS earned her M.A. in Home Economics from the University of Washington with an emphasis in family relationships. From her background in teaching and eleven years experience as a grandmother, she presents an easy-to-follow, practical, and inspiring Bible study.

She has also contributed to thirteen books and has written hundreds of articles, devotionals, book reviews, and personal experience stories. Focus on the Family's *Clubhouse* magazines for children publish Lydia's recipes, which she develops and tests with her grandchildren. Her bimonthly column, "A Cup of Tea with Lydia," appears in *The Country Register* papers in the United States and Canada with a readership of nearly 3/4 million. (Hence her grandchildren call her "Grandma Tea.") In 2000, her writing earned her the "Writer of the Year" award from Oregon Christian Writers, and she teaches at writers' conferences.

Most importantly, Lydia loves God and her family. Her passion for prayer and passing the baton of faith to future generations resonates throughout her life and writing. She has been active in Moms In Touch International and has prayed weekly with other mothers, and now grandmothers, for more than twenty years. She also organizes bimonthly family prayer times for her extended family.

Together, Lydia and her husband Milt are intentional about passing on a legacy of faith to their two married children and five grandchildren. They are active members of Northshore Baptist Church in Bothell, Washington, and live in the Seattle area. More information can be found at: www.PreparingMyHeart.net.

Introduction

Ready or Not, Here I Come!

Who hasn't played the childhood game Hide-and-Seek? Everyone looks for a place to hide while one person counts and at last calls out, "Ready or not, here I come!"

This game reminds me of how it feels to become a grandparent. When our daughter told us she and her husband were expecting our first grandchild, I said, "I'm not ready to be a grandmother!"

"Then get ready," she said. "You still have months to prepare."

I had always wanted to be a grandmother, but the reality of becoming one caught me off guard. Like the game Hide-and-Seek, this was a "ready or not, here I come" experience.

My excitement mounted as I anticipated the birth of this child. And when our daughter called at 2 a.m. to say she was in labor and on her way to the hospital, we hurried there to await our grandchild's birth.

When Peter, our rosy-cheeked grandson, arrived, I took one look at him, and he grabbed my heart forever. Even though I didn't know all that my new role involved, I knew I loved this precious gift from God to our family.

Now, eleven years and five wonderful grandchildren later, I know grandparenting is an exciting and important responsibility. I've also learned a few things I wish I had known before I became a grandparent. I wrote this Bible study to help you prepare your heart for this significant role. And if you're already a grandparent, I pray this study will help you become the best one you can be.

Grandchildren come, ready or not! So let's get ready!

Happy grandparenting,

Lydia (aka Grandma Tea)

Contents

Prepare for a New Role

(Beyond spoiling grandkids and sending them home)

When our young grandchildren come to visit, they greet us with gleeful hugs and then run to the playroom to find their favorite toys. Four-year-old Owen often plays with the kaleidoscope. He peers through the hole on one end, spins the wheel at the other, and watches the colorful shapes form different designs.

As we begin this study, we'll look through our grandparenting kaleidoscopes and discover what the Bible says about our new roles and responsibilities. We'll spin the wheel each day and watch different patterns emerge as we consider these aspects of grandparenting:

Day One	God's View of Children
Day Two	Relating to Adult Children
Day Three	Roles with Grandchildren
Day Four	Sharing Grandparenting
Day Five	Forgiveness in Grandparenting

Like young grandchildren rummaging through a toy chest for favorite toys, we'll dig into God's Word and find treasures to apply in grandparenting.

God's View of Children

Bill and Ruth longed to become grandparents. Though their three children were married, none had children yet. Finally, Ruth proudly announced, "We're going to be grandparents!"

Debbie's children weren't married, so she had no thoughts of becoming a grandmother. As a widow, she struggled to adjust to the loss of her husband and to her role as a single parent. When her unmarried teenage daughter became pregnant, Debbie's heart sank. "I wasn't expecting to become a grandmother so soon or under those circumstances."

Marla's son married, and in a few years she became a grandmother of two. Several years later, her son divorced, and her grandchildren lived with their mother on the other side of the state. Marla seldom saw them. Then her son remarried a woman with two children. Suddenly, she became a stepgrandmother to grade-school-aged granddaughters who lived nearby. "I felt uncertain about my new role," she said.

Julie's son and his wife seemingly couldn't have children, so they adopted a baby girl from China. Julie wrote, "We have a China doll!" Later Julie's daughter-in-law became pregnant and gave Ravenna a baby brother. After that, they adopted a child with special needs—another "China doll."

Although circumstances differ, these individuals all received new titles and faced new roles as grandparents. What *is* a grandparent's role? For years my friend Donna, who has twenty-four grandchildren, had a plaque with the following words hanging in her kitchen:

Grandma's Rules

Feed cookies
Give presents
Send kids home to Mom and Dad

We smile when we read these words. But seriously, is there more to grandparenting than spoiling the grandkids? What can we learn from the Bible about our duties as grandparents?

Although God's Word doesn't include a section called "Crash Course in Grandparenting," it is filled with wisdom for grandparenting. As you examine the passages in this study, you'll find the Bible teaches much about preparing our hearts to become grandparents after God's own heart.

Heartwork

The gospels of Matthew, Mark, and Luke give us glimpses of how Jesus views children. We'll read two of these parallel passages:

> *Then little children were brought to Jesus for him to place his hands on them and pray for them. But the disciples rebuked those who brought them. Jesus said, "Let the little children come to me, and do not hinder them, for the kingdom of heaven belongs to such as these." When he had placed his hands on them, he went on from there.* (Matthew 19:13–15)

> *Then they brought little children to Him, that He might touch them; but the disciples rebuked those who brought them. But when Jesus saw it, He was greatly displeased and said to them, "Let the little children come to Me, and do not forbid them; for of such is the kingdom of God. Assuredly, I say to you, whoever does not receive the kingdom of God as a little child will by no means enter it." And He took them up in His arms, laid His hands on them, and blessed them.* (Mark 10:13–16 NKJV)

1. Underline Jesus' actions. What do His words and actions reveal about His view of children?

_____

_____

_____

_____

Have you seen pictures in Bible storybooks of Jesus holding small children on His lap? When I consider how Jesus welcomed little children, I almost wish I had lived during Bible times. Then I could have brought my grandchildren to Him for a blessing. Even though we don't live during those days, we can still carry our grandchildren—born or unborn—to Him in prayer and daily ask Him to bless them.

The mothers who brought their children to Jesus must have felt encouraged when they saw how Jesus loved children, felt compassion for them, and blessed them.

2. Look at the passages again. In contrast to Jesus, how did the disciples respond to the children?

_____

_____

_____

3. What do you think the disciples said when they rebuked those who brought children to Jesus? What tone of voice might they have used?

_____

_____

_____

4. Check the phrases that might describe the disciples' thoughts and feelings.

_____ Children are too much trouble.

_____ We have more important things to do.

_____ Children are precious.

_____ Send them away.

_____ Children are nuisances.

_____ The children will bother Jesus.

_____ Jesus doesn't have time for children.

_____ Children are fun to be with.

Jesus was displeased with the disciples' actions. From my viewpoint, they deserved Jesus' correction.

Although I find it easy to criticize the disciples' response to children, sometimes I become frustrated or impatient with my grandchildren. Perhaps, at times you feel your views or actions toward your grandchildren are more like the disciples' behavior than Jesus' welcoming embrace. And maybe your new role seems daunting.

5. How did you view the prospect of becoming a grandparent? Were you eager? Apprehensive? Somewhere in between? Describe your feelings and response.

_____

_____

_____

_____

6. Now that we have the privilege of grandparenting, let's look at Jesus as our model. Jesus said, *"Let the little children come to me"* (Matthew 19:14). How can you let the little children come to you? Here are a few suggestions to help you get started. Add ideas of your own.

- Open my heart to them
- Make time in my life for them
- Hold and cuddle them
- Cherish and treasure them
- Pray for them
- _____
- _____

> *I know my grandma loves me because she makes custard for me when I come over."*
> Clara, age 6

Other passages in the Bible tell of God's love for children. For example, Psalm 127:3 affirms the value of children: *"Sons are a heritage from the LORD, children a reward from him."*

Notice the verse says children are *rewards*, not nuisances. A reward is something good given to us, a prize. Grandchildren are a gift. *"Don't you see that children are GOD's best gift?"* (Psalm 127:3 MSG).

GRAND Thought: Jesus loves and values children. That means our grandchildren are precious to Him, and they are God's gifts to us.

Prayer: Lord Jesus, thank You for showing us Your heart of love toward children. You truly are a loving God. Thank You for the gift of my children and grandchildren. Help me become so much like You that I wholeheartedly welcome children into my life. Show me areas where I need to change so I can become the grandparent You want me to be. Please help me to gratefully and joyfully make room in my heart and home for the grandchildren You give me. I want to grow in my relationship with them and with You. May Your love flow through me to my precious grandchildren, born and unborn.

Journal your thoughts about how God has spoken to you through this lesson.

_____

_____

_____

_____

Today we'll spin our grandparenting kaleidoscopes again and see another aspect of our roles—relating to our grown children, the parents of our grandchildren. When our children marry, our relationships with them change. After they give birth to our grandchildren, our relationships change even more. As parents, how should we relate to grown children who are *now also parents*?

Grandma Leona said, "We need to always be the parents—but not be parenting. We maintain the position of mothers or fathers while learning to relate as adults to adults."

Grandma Ruth said, "Grandparenting really begins when you are raising your children. How you train and build relationships with them will influence how you will relate to your children when you're grandparents."

We can't go back and change previous relationships with our children, but, with God's help, we can strengthen present relationships and move forward.

Heartwork

As I interviewed grandparents, one sticky point of tension came up often: What can grandparents say and do to assist in raising their grandchildren? In other words, who's in charge of the grandkids?

Let's look at Genesis 2:24 to see God's plan for the family from the beginning: *"For this reason a man will leave his father and mother and be united to his wife, and they will become one flesh."*

1. According to this verse, what should our adult children do when they marry?

_____

How does that change our relationship with them?

_____

_____

The King James Version says our children should "leave" us and "cleave" to their spouses. They form new family units, and our task is to release them to do so and support them in their new life.

First, we release our children in marriage, and then, if they have children, we face the next step of releasing—not interfering as they raise our grandchildren. Although it's tempting to speak from experience and tell them what to do, let's remember that our children are learning on the job, just as we did as inexperienced parents. Besides, God's Word says, *"Children, obey your parents"* (Ephesians 6:1; Colossians 3:20), not "obey your *grandparents.*"

Perhaps you're thinking, *You mean I can't tell my kids how to parent?* Recall your days as a new parent. Did you want your parents telling you what to do? According to seasoned grandparents, telling our kids how to raise their kids is a no-no. Listen to these grandparents' advice:

"The most difficult thing as a grandparent is trying to surrender my grandchildren to the Lord. I am not their parent. I cannot 'fix' their folks; they rarely appreciate my interfering in their parenting, especially in front of the grandkids. But I take great comfort in the way God preserved my children in spite of my mistakes and character flaws. I must trust He is willing to do the same with my grandchildren." Grandma Debbie

> *Find out how involved the parents want you to be, and respect their boundaries. Allow the new parents to parent the way they want, not giving advice unless they ask for it."*
> *Grandma Shirley*

"I don't always agree with my kids' parenting techniques, but I *must* remember they are the parents and need me to back them up." Grandma Lynnette

"We should take our lead from the parent: how to discipline, how to 'spoil,' what is okay, and what is not okay; never belittling the parents; not providing what the grandparent needs but what the children and parents need." Grandma Dianna

We need to accept our changing roles. We were coaches—guiding and training our kids, but now we move to the sidelines (GRANDstands) and become their cheerleaders. Even though we can't do some things as grandparents, there are many things we *can* do.

Let's look at three positive ways to relate to our grown children: encourage them, offer support, and pray.

Encourage

2. As you read 1 Thessalonians 5:11, underline the two verbs that tell us what to do:

> *Therefore encourage one another and build each other up, just as in fact you are doing.*

> *We try to encourage our children in their parenting styles and cautiously give advice when we think it would be appreciated." Grandma Sylvia*

3. In your relationship with your adult children, list three ways you can encourage them and build them up as they parent your grandchildren.

_____

_____

_____

_____

4. Through our words and actions, we can encourage or discourage our children. Read the following verses to find out how, and fill in the other columns. Not all answers are found directly in the verses, so include your own thoughts.

Scripture	Do	Don't	Why?
When words are many, sin is not absent, but he who holds his tongue is wise. (Proverbs 10:19)			
Everyone should be quick to listen, slow to speak and slow to become angry, for man's anger does not bring about the righteous life that God desires. (James 1:19, 20)			
Speaking the truth in love, we will in all things grow up into him who is the Head, that is, Christ. (Ephesians 4:15)			

5. How can we apply these dos and don'ts in grandparenting? In what situations would it be wise to hold our tongues?

_____

_____

_____

Other grandparents suggested:

- Ask God to help you guard your mouth and show you what to say and not say.
- Show respect, and give your children credit for being good parents.
- Treat your grown children as adults.

It's been said God gave us two ears and one mouth for a reason. For myself, I need to listen more and talk less.

> *I've allowed each of our three daughters and their husbands to parent in their own styles, knowing their personalities and gifts are unique to them. I praise and encourage them every time possible."*
> *Grandma Shirley*

Support

If you're a "doer" and are eager to get involved, I caution you to proceed carefully. Seek God's direction and ask your children how involved they want you to become. This varies from person to person and can change with time and circumstances. One size doesn't fit all.

6. Recall the birth of your first child. How did you feel as a new parent? Circle the number that indicates where you were on this continuum:

Scared—1——2——3——4——5——6——7——8——9——10—Confident

I felt scared, unprepared, and inadequate. As the youngest in a family of eight, I had never taken care of younger siblings, had no experience babysitting, and didn't play with baby dolls. Then this darling but fussy baby girl arrived. I wasn't sure what to do. So whenever she cried, I cried, too—with real tears and cries of "Help!" to the Creator. God did help me, and our daughter is now a wonderful forty-year-old mother of two of our grandsons.

Step into your children's shoes. How might they feel in their parenting roles? Unsure of themselves? Or confident? How can you be supportive? Support may *not* include telling them what to do, unless they ask. Instead, give them hugs, affirming words, and practical help with meals, housework, and child care so they can rest.

Our children also need space to learn from their mistakes. In time, they will grow into their new roles and may even become better parents than we were.

Grandma Dianna says, "Grandparents, especially grandmas, can be resources and encourage mothers who are struggling at different stages of life. For example: a colicky baby, potty training, or a smart-alecky teen only lasts so long. Grandmas can empathize with the mothers and yet reassure them it will pass. They can pray for that stage of the children's lives, maybe give hints, or just be quiet and listen."

> *W*e keep our grand- children one weekend each month to give our children time to themselves."
> Grandma Carole

7. Let's read Paul's instructions in Galatians 6:2 about offering help: *"Carry each other's burdens, and in this way you will fulfill the law of Christ."*

What does God say we're doing when we help others?

_____

_____

Although Paul says, *"Carry each other's burdens"* in Galatians 6:2, in verse 5 he writes, *"Each one should carry his own load,"* or in the King James Version, *"Every man shall bear his own burden."* At first this sounds contradictory, but it isn't.

The word for "burden" in Galatians 6:2 is *baros*, and the word for "load" in Galatians 6:5 is *phortion*. *Baros* "denotes a weight, anything pressing on one physically or that makes a demand on one's resources, whether material or spiritual." It always refers to "what is heavy or burdensome." But *phortion* refers to "something carried . . . to be borne, without reference to its weight" (*Expository Dictionary of New Testament Words* by W. E. Vine, 1:157 [4 vols]).

I once heard the difference explained this way: We each have our own load (like a backpack) to carry. But when heavy burdens come, we need help. During difficult seasons, our adult children may need assistance to carry their burdens.

Grandma Donna said, "Years ago, when I was going through a difficult time, my heart was hardened by fear, bitterness, and resentment. But the Lord gave me Ezekiel 36:26 as a promise to soften my heart toward my family: *'I will give you a new heart and put a new spirit in you; I will remove from you your heart of stone and give you a heart of flesh.'* God changed me from an uptight, fearful mom to a faith-filled woman who does have a heart of flesh that hurts when my kids hurt and is filled with joy when they are content."

> *I am their encourager, prayer warrior, and 'relief pitcher' when they need care or support."*
> Grandma Leona

Pray

Prayer is the most important way to support our children. Consider Paul's fatherly words to Timothy: *"To Timothy, my dear son: Grace, mercy and peace from God the Father and Christ Jesus our Lord. I thank God, whom I serve, as my forefathers did, with a clear conscience, as night and day I constantly remember you in my prayers. Recalling your tears, I long to see you, so that I may be filled with joy"* (2 Timothy 1:2–4).

I love the tenderness of Paul's words to Timothy. In *The Message* it says, "Every time I say your name in prayer—which is practically all the time—I thank God for you." Paul's constant prayers for Timothy encourage me to pray often for my adult children.

8. In what areas do your children need prayer? If you need starter ideas, write one or two of these on a 3x5 card, and use it as a bookmark to remind you to pray for:

- A growing, happy marriage (Malachi 2:15; Hebrews 13:4)
- Humble, teachable hearts (1 Peter 5:6)
- God's blessing on their home (Numbers 6:24–26)
- Gratitude and contentment (1 Thessalonians 5:18)
- God's guidance in training their children (Proverbs 22:6; Ephesians 6:4)
- Their trust in God to grow. They won't lean on their own understanding (Proverbs 3:5)

- Your specific desires and requests

_____

As we pray for our adult children, we can also ask God to help our relationship with them to continue to grow.

9. Consider ways you'd like to grow in your relationship with your adult child(ren). Then write your prayer here.

Lord, help me to be more

_____

_____

_____

I would like my relationship with my grown kids to be more

_____

_____

_____

Be assured—God hears your sincere prayers and will honor them.

> *It's a grand thing to be a parent of a parent. That's why we're called GRANDparents.*

Grandma Cheryl's words sum up the need to encourage, support, and pray for our children: "Unconditional love and support of the new parents of your grandchildren should be paramount, along with generous and frequent doses of praise and affirmation. Instead of fretting and worrying, pray, pray, pray, and leave the outcome with God!"

GRAND Thought: Our role with our adult children need not be puzzling. If we ask, God will gladly show us ways to please both Him and them.

Prayer: Heavenly Father, I'm excited to become a grandparent, but I'm also a little anxious about my role. Do I know what to do? Fill my heart with overflowing love for my grandchild. And help me build a stronger relationship with my grandchild's parents as together we anticipate a new life. Prepare me for this important role. As my grandchild grows, help me grow spiritually and wait patiently for this dear child You are forming.

"You're going to be a grandparent!" Do you remember where you were when you heard the exciting news? With that announcement, your life changed forever. Perhaps you called a friend with the news, rushed out to buy a brag book, or imagined cuddling your new grandbaby. But after the initial excitement, maybe you wondered, "What's my role?"

If you're not sure of your job description, perhaps this ad will help you determine yours. It was written by a mother of toddlers to entice her parents to move closer to them.

<u>Help Wanted</u>

Opening: Full-time Grandparent

Job Description:

- Storyteller
- Shark and Spider Impersonator
- Must excel in the art of "Hide-and-Seek"
- French fry sharer and ice cream giver
- Go to park at least weekly. At the park, you can push swings, catch kids at the bottom of slides, fly kites, kick soccer balls, etc.
- Attend sporting and special events with young children
- Provide special sleepovers and spoil kids with treats their parents forbid
- Snuggle kids at bedtime after prayers
- Provide occasional kid-sitting so their parents can have a date

Pay: Hugs, kisses, and filling kids with a lifetime of memories that will imprint them forever

A.K.A.: Leaving a legacy (<u>PRICELESS</u>)

Would that motivate you to move closer to your grandkids? The grandparents who received this help-wanted ad yearned to fill the vacancy soon.

Heartwork

Now let's turn to the book of "Grandparenting" to gain biblical wisdom. In my Bible, it's on page—wait a minute. You know there's no such book. Don't you wish there were? Still, we can glean biblical principles and apply them to grandparenting.

1. The grandparents I contacted listed these actions as part of their roles. Check three you consider important.

_____ Love   _____ Pray
_____ Guide   _____ Offer child care
_____ Model   _____ Spend time with them
_____ Encourage   _____ Always be there for them
_____ Teach   _____ Attend activities
_____ Affirm

We'll focus on love—the role most frequently mentioned by grandparents. This broad topic spans the Bible from Genesis to Revelation and is used nearly seven hundred times in the New International Version. You might say the Bible is all about love.

Most of the time, the word *love* describes relationships: God's love for us, our love for God, and our love for others. The Greek New Testament word for God's love is *agape*. It's unconditional love. We don't need to earn it. Let's briefly look at God's love for us and His command to love others. Then we'll finish this lesson by learning practical ways to love our grandchildren.

> *What took me by surprise was the deep love I felt for my first grandchild. Now I have a better understanding of how deep and rich God's love is for me."* Grandma Bonnie

God's Love for Us

2. Read the following verses about God's love and fill in the blanks to describe it. Keep in mind how we can show love to our grandchildren.

But because of his great love for us, God, who is rich in mercy, made us alive with Christ even when we were dead in transgressions. (Ephesians 2:4, 5)

God's love is _____

How priceless is your unfailing love! Both high and low among men find refuge in the shadow of your wings. (Psalm 36:7)

God's love is _____

For I am convinced that neither death nor life, neither angels nor demons, neither the present nor the future, nor any powers, neither height nor depth, nor anything else in all creation, will be able to separate us from the love of God that is in Christ Jesus our Lord. (Romans 8:38, 39)

God's love is _____

How great is the love the Father has lavished on us, that we should be called children of God! (1 John 3:1)

God's love is _____

Take time to thank God for His wonderful love for your grandchildren and for you.

Our Love for Others

If Christ dwells in our hearts, the Holy Spirit can give us unconditional love for others.

3. As you read the following verses, underline each "love one another" (or "each other") and write your insights in the chart. In the third column, apply these insights to grandparenting.

"Love One Another" Verses	Insights about Love	Apply to Grandparenting
May the Lord make your love increase and overflow for each other and for everyone else, just as ours does for you. (1 Thessalonians 3:12)		
Now that you have purified yourselves by obeying the truth so that you have sincere love for your brothers, love one another deeply, from the heart. (1 Peter 1:22)		
Dear friends, since God so loved us, we also ought to love one another. (1 John 4:11)		

Love is the foundation of our relationship with our grandchildren. But even sweet-smelling, cuddly grandchildren are born with sin natures and aren't always easy to love. How can we pattern our love for them after God's love? Let's consider specific ways.

In *The Five Love Languages of Children* (Chicago, IL: Northfield Publishing, 1997), Gary Chapman and Ross Campbell identify five ways to express love to children. The authors believe each child has a primary love language but that every child benefits from all of these:

- Physical Touch
- Words of Affirmation
- Quality Time
- Gifts
- Acts of Service

4. The following examples show how Grandma Sharon demonstrates her love. List the love language each one shows.

- My four- and five-year-old grandsons beam when I praise them. _____
- My independent eighteen-year-old granddaughter still likes to cuddle. (She grew up on it.) _____
- My fourteen-year-old grandson thanks me when I help him with homeschooling. _____
- My granddaughters love to scrapbook with me.
  _____
- My ten-year-old granddaughter loves to make and give little gifts and cards. We make them together.
  _____

If you have more than one grandchild, maybe you've wondered why one loves your hugs and kisses and the other doesn't. Perhaps it's related to their primary love languages. One of my grandchildren has a strong need for physical touch, while another values quality time. And all kids love gifts!

Young children need all these expressions of love. As they grow older, preferences emerge, but these may change over time. Also realize their love language may be different from yours.

> *O*ur grandkids love us and think we are very special in spite of wrinkles, skin tags, and age spots." Grandma Sharon

Observe your grandchildren to discover which type of love they prefer.

The Bible includes verses that emphasize these love languages:

Physical Touch

And they brought young children to him,
that he should touch them. (Mark 10:13 KJV)

Words of Affirmation

The tongue has the power of life and death,
and those who love it will eat its fruit.
(Proverbs 18:21)

Quality Time

I long to see you . . . that you
and I may be mutually encouraged by each other's faith.
(Romans 1:11, 12)

Gifts

I have received full payment and even more; I am amply sup-
plied, now that I have received from Epaphroditus the gifts you
sent. They are a fragrant offering, an acceptable sacrifice, pleas-
ing to God. (Philippians 4:18)

Acts of Service

Dear children, let's not merely say that we love each other; let us
show the truth by our actions. (1 John 3:18 NLT)

5. If you're already a grandparent, think about a specific grandchild as you list one or more ways to express love in each love language. If you're not a grandparent yet, list ideas for how you could show love in these ways to future grandchildren.

- Physical Touch _____
- Words of Affirmation _____
- Quality Time _____
- Gifts _____
- Acts of Service _____

6. No matter what love language you use, glean from these grandparents' wisdom. Highlight examples you can apply.

"As a grandparent, my responsibility is different, so I have more freedom to simply enjoy them. Grandpa gets to play dolls, and Grandma goes on nature hikes in the woods and looks at bugs!" Grandma Jeanne

> *Y es indeedy, grandkids are the best thing I ever did. Grandkids keep old people alive and laughing." Grandma Petey* 🐢

"Our grandkids love the toy box we keep in the garage for when they visit. We provide basketballs for the hoop on the back patio, too. The tea parties are also a hit. I use good china and the silver teapot and buy special cookies or a decorated cake to add to the ambience." Grandma Sylvia

"Take time to love all your children and grandchildren equally. Grandchildren know when you are really interested in them, and they know when you've shown genuine love." Grandpa Bill

"I volunteer in my grandchildren's public school classrooms. I enjoy it and they are proud their grandma helps at school. I also teach Sunday school. My teenage grandson said, 'Grandma, you are my favorite teacher. You show love to everyone and make the class fun.'" Grandma Dianna

"Don't major on minors, especially when dealing with teenagers. Keep the *big* picture in mind, not all the little side issues. Be aware of which priorities are really important to your family. Children don't care about a fancy home but instead want a safe, loving home." Grandma Barbara

"Since I live a long distance from all my grandkids, I send them e-mail messages. Skye (five years old) particularly asks if Grandma has sent her an e-mail. I also send birthday e-cards,

---

Great-Grandma Margaret shares these eight tips:

1. *Really listen.*
2. *Give lots of hugs.*
3. *Do fun things together and encourage creativity. Build special memories geared individually to the grandchild's unique personality.*
4. *Correct only when absolutely necessary (but be firm when needed).*
5. *Teach, when it comes graciously, but never, never preach! We can share our faith spontaneously without preaching.*
6. *Attend their programs and sports events whenever possible.*
7. *Write notes for no reason except to share your love and interest in the child's life.*
8. *Pray with them on any and all issues that concern them when it's natural and spontaneous to do so. Don't force or ever presume!* 🐢

which are a hit. When my grandchildren come to visit, I make homemade pizza. I don't think it compares to purchased pizza, but the grandkids lap it up and ask for more." Grandma Sylvia

GRAND Thought: The title of Grandpa or Grandma comes with an enormous privilege and responsibility. To build a lifelong relationship with your grandchildren, start at their birth, and love them from your heart for the rest of your life. Remember, once a grandparent, always a grandparent.

Prayer: Heavenly Father, thank You for the privilege of grandparenting. Please show me how to best love my grandchildren. Let Your boundless, sacrificial love flow through me to them. And I pray that my grandchildren and I will have the power to *"grasp how wide and long and high and deep"* Your love is and to know it surpasses knowledge.

(Based on Ephesians 3:18, 19)

Record special thoughts or insights to apply to your situation.

_____

_____

_____

_____

_____

Sharing Grandparenting

Day Four

The phone rang in the middle of the night, jarring me awake. "Hi, Mom. The baby is coming," our daughter said.

Now wide awake, I woke my groggy husband, and we hurried to the hospital. (I don't know why we were in such a hurry, because the baby wasn't.) As my husband and I waited, we prayed for a healthy baby and a safe delivery.

Before long, our son-in-law's parents arrived, and together we waited for our grandchild's birth. The ultrasound had shown a boy, but I wanted the official word before announcing my grandson. After an eternity of waiting, a tired, blurry-eyed new father came out and announced, "It's a boy! Peter is here."

And with Peter's birth, new grandparents were born, too. As Milt and I stepped into the room to meet our first grandchild, we also stepped into a new stage of life. One look at Peter, and it was love at first sight.

We all took turns holding Peter. When it was my turn to cuddle him, I studied the shape of his cute little nose; held his soft, tiny hand; and thanked God for my precious grandson. God had done it again—He had created another child in His image. "Lord, let him become a child of God, too," I whispered in my heart.

Heartwork

Though my husband and I lacked experience in grandparenting, we felt enthused about our new role. But it wasn't ours alone. From the start, it also belonged to another set of grandparents. Today's lesson will focus on our relationship with the other grandparents who share this role.

1. Read Proverbs 17:6, which mentions three generations and their relationships to each other: *"Children's children are a crown to the aged, and parents are the pride of their children."*

Fill in your family names to show the family tree for one grandchild.

Aged (grandparents)

_____ and _____

Children (your children; parents of grandchildren)

_____ and _____

Children's children (grandchild)

_____

2. According to this verse, how do children feel about their parents?

_____

_____

What are grandchildren called? _____

From God's viewpoint, at our grandson's birth, a coronation took place. We were crowned grandparents! After your grandchild's birth, you'll wear a crown, too.

3. Why do you think God called grandchildren *"crowns to the aged"*?

_____

_____

_____

When we realize God sees our grandchildren as valuable crowns, it validates the significance of our grandparenting roles.

4. Psalm 128 gives another view of grandchildren. As you read this psalm, underline the words *blessed* and *blessings*.

> *Blessed are all who fear the LORD, who walk in his ways.*
> *You will eat the fruit of your labor; blessings and prosperity will be yours.*
> *Your wife will be like a fruitful vine within your house; your sons will be like olive shoots around your table.*
> *Thus is the man blessed who fears the LORD.*
> *May the LORD bless you from Zion all the days of your life; may you see the prosperity of Jerusalem,*
> *and may you live to see your children's children.*

5. In this passage, whom does God bless, and what are the prerequisites of being blessed?

_____

_____

6. How does God bless those who fear Him?

_____

_____

_____

_____

In Psalm 128:6, we learn that our blessings include living to see our grandchildren. Do you think of your grandchildren as blessings?

As we grow older, it's a joy to see our family tree grow and see our lives extended through our grandchildren. Together with the other grandparents, we can nurture, love, and encourage our children and grandchildren.

Grandma Ruth said, "When our daughter-in-law traveled to London, her parents came and stayed with our son and family to care for the children. It's great to share the opportunities and responsibilities with the other grandparents."

But there's potential for friction in all relationships, including our shared grandparenting role.

Since we're imperfect, we may become jealous, competitive, or judgmental in our shared responsibilities. These attitudes can poison our relationships not only with the other grandparents but also with our children and grandchildren.

Antidotes are available for specific poisons our grandchildren might get into. But what's the antidote to control poisonous attitudes? Immediately call on God through prayer, and then check His Word.

7. Read the chart on the adjoining page, and check the attitudes you struggle with.

Here are additional tips to keep unhealthy attitudes from spreading:

- Identify wrong attitudes as soon as they begin (Psalm 139:23).
- Take hold of your thoughts and confess wrong attitudes to God (Psalm 51:10; 2 Corinthians 10:5; 1 John 1:9).
- Cleanse your heart of unhealthy attitudes by immersing yourself in God's Word (Psalm 119:11).
- Write helpful verses on note cards, and read them when you struggle with sinful attitudes (Deuteronomy 11:18, 20).
- Thank God for the other grandparents, look for the positive contributions they make, and pray for them (Ephesians 1:16, 17).

8. When I asked experienced grandparents for advice on relating to the other grandparents, they shared these ideas. Check those meaningful to you.

"Remember you are not competing with the other grandparents. Just appreciate who you are and what you can add to the family." Grandma Joann

"Families have their own DNA, and there are many

> *When the grandkids come over, they like to talk about the fun they've had with their other grandparents. Clara will sometimes say, "You know Grammy and Poppy, too, don't you?" I make it a point to reply, "Yes, I know them, and they are wonderful people. I'm glad you have two sets of grandparents who love you so much."—Grandma Tea*

> **We take captive every thought to make it obedient to Christ.**
> **(2 Corinthians 10:5)**

Getting Along with the Other Grandparents

Poisonous Attitudes	Symptoms	God's Antidote	Treatment
1. Jealous	I envy the other grandparents and the fun they have with our grandkids.	*Let us behave decently . . . not in dissension and jealousy.* (Romans 13:13)	Replace jealousy with gratitude. *"Give thanks in all circumstances"* (1 Thessalonians 5:18). Lord, forgive my jealousy and give me a **grateful** heart.
2. Competitive	I want to be my grandchild's favorite grandparent.	*For by the grace given me I say to every one of you: Do not think of yourself more highly than you ought, but rather think of yourself with sober judgment.* (Romans 12:3)	Replace competing with sharing. *"So in Christ we who are many form one body, and each member belongs to all the others"* (Romans 12:5). Lord, show me ways to **partner** with the other grandparents and not compete.
3. Comparing	I think the other grandparents spend too much (or too little) time with the grandkids.	*We do not dare to classify or compare ourselves with some who commend themselves. When they measure themselves by themselves and compare themselves with themselves, they are not wise.* (2 Corinthians 10:12)	Replace comparing with affirming. *"Honor one another above yourselves"* (Romans 12:10). Lord, help me to **honor** the other grandparents in thoughts and actions.
4. Controlling	I don't want the other grandparents to spend so much money on gifts for the grandkids.	*Each of you should look not only to your own interests, but also to the interests of others.* (Philippians 2:4)	Replace controlling with supporting. *"Submit to one another out of reverence for Christ"* (Ephesians 5:21). Lord, forgive my controlling ways, and show me how to be **supportive**.
5. Judging	I think the other grandparents are poor role models and are too critical.	*"Do not judge, or you too will be judged."* (Matthew 7:1)	Replace judgment with acceptance. *"Accept one another, then, just as Christ accepted you, in order to bring praise to God"* (Romans 15:7). Lord, forgive me for judging. Help me **accept** the other grandparents and pray for them.
6. Quarrelsome	I disagree with the other grandparents' behavior and values and want to set them straight.	*Don't have anything to do with foolish and stupid arguments, because you know they produce quarrels. And the Lord's servant must not quarrel; instead, he must be kind to everyone, able to teach, not resentful.* (2 Timothy 2:23, 24)	Replace quarreling with peace. *"Let the peace of Christ rule in your hearts"* (Colossians 3:15). Lord, forgive me for quarreling and arguing, and help me become a peacemaker.

acceptable ways to accomplish tasks. Get to know the other set of grandparents, honor them, and affirm their different gifts.

> Create in me a pure heart, O God, and renew a steadfast spirit within me. (Psalm 51:10)

When values differ, demonstrating your values will go further than trying to correct theirs." Grandpa Gord

"If possible, be friends with the other grandparents. Get together for dinner, and include them in celebrations when appropriate. In all things be kind, loving, accepting, and encouraging. If they live far from their grandchildren, send photos of grandkids, or even write to them. If there are disagreements or problems, always bring water, not wood, to the fire." Grandma Ruth

"We need to honor our son and daughter-in-law's parents to their faces, behind their backs, and to their adult children. When it comes to holidays and special experiences, we need to share the time—not hog it for ourselves. If we understand the uniqueness of their families, it will help us understand their parenting." Grandma Leona

"View the other grandparents as a plus and tell them how much you appreciate them. Be glad when they are included in family gatherings." Grandma Petey

All relationships require God's grace. Thankfully, God has plenty to share: *"My grace is sufficient for you, for my power is made perfect in weakness"* (2 Corinthians 12:9).

GRAND Thought: If we *compete* with the other grandparents, everyone loses, and we diminish the impact they and we can have on our grandchildren. But if we pull together rather than apart, God can use us to *complete* the work He wants to do in our grandchildren's lives.

Prayer: Heavenly Father, thank You for allowing me to live long enough to see Psalm 128 fulfilled in my life—to see my children's children. Help me grandparent them in ways that please You. Pour out Your grace in my life so I can honor others above myself. Especially help me guard my attitudes and conquer ungodly ones. Help me develop and nurture a positive relationship with the other grandparents. Let Your peace rule in my heart and in every area of my life.

Add your prayer:

_____

_____

_____

_____

_____

Forgiveness in Grandparenting

This week we've spun our kaleidoscopes and examined our roles with adult children, grandchildren, and the other grandparents. These new relationships provide many opportunities to give and receive forgiveness. Here are some situations where grandparents found it hard to forgive themselves and others:

"I see things we didn't do very well with our kids that are being repeated with our grandkids."

"I don't always agree with my kids' parenting techniques."

"I like the grandkids to get along. It upsets me when they fight with each other."

"My teenage granddaughter doesn't always choose God's ways."

"The other grandparents hog the grandkids."

Heartwork

These are only a few examples of times when forgiveness is needed. Forgiveness is easy to receive but hard to give. I want others to forgive me. But in my own strength, I don't always want to forgive others. Do you find it hard to forgive or to ask others to forgive you?

No one said forgiveness would be easy. But it's necessary. When Jesus taught the disciples to pray, He included forgiveness as part of His model prayer. Look at Matthew 6:12 in the Lord's Prayer, which deals with forgiveness: *"Forgive us our debts, as we forgive our debtors"* (KJV).

1. According to this verse, who needs to be forgiven?

_____

_____

2. And who does the forgiving?
Of us: _____
Of our debtors: _____
Two other Bible versions say it this way:

> *Keep us forgiven with you and forgiving others.* (MSG)

> *And forgive us our debts, as we also have forgiven (left, remitted, and let go of the debts, and have given up resentment against) our debtors.* (AMP)

The Amplified Version describes forgiveness as sincere and complete. God forgives us completely, and we are to let go of the resentments we feel toward others. It's not like the flippant "sorry" we say when playing the Sorry! board game with our grandkids. In that game, although we say "sorry," we aren't. Instead, we're glad when players have to go back spaces and get behind. Each player's goal is to win. But in real life, forgiving one another is a win-win situation. Each person wins when forgiveness is offered and accepted. Winning spiritually means to forgive and be forgiven.

3. The two verses that follow Jesus' model prayer teach more about forgiveness. Underline the words and phrases that indicate the conditions for receiving forgiveness.

> *For if you forgive men when they sin against you, your heavenly Father will also forgive you. But if you do not forgive men their sins, your Father will not forgive your sins.* (Matthew 6:14, 15)

At first these verses troubled me. Why? Because being forgiven by God is linked with forgiving others. But the passage does not mean our salvation is based on forgiving others. We cannot earn salvation. It's a free gift: *"For it is by grace you have been saved, through faith—and this not from yourselves, it is the gift of God—not by works, so that no one can boast"* (Ephesians 2:8, 9). However, when we are unwilling to forgive others, our day-to-day fellowship with God is broken.

The Lord's Prayer includes a request for daily bread. Likewise, to remain in fellowship with God, we need to ask for forgiveness each day—to keep short accounts with God and others.

4. Even though Jesus died for all our sins and He forgives us when we ask, why might we be slow (or unwilling) to forgive others? Check the statements you have heard or thought.

> "Lord, how many times shall I forgive my brother when he sins against me? Up to seven times?" Jesus answered, "I tell you, not seven times, but seventy-seven times." (Matthew 18:21, 22)

_____ I think my sins aren't as serious as those committed against me.

_____ They don't deserve to be forgiven.

_____ They haven't asked for forgiveness, so I don't need to forgive them.

_____ Even if I forgive her, she'll do it again.

_____ If I forgive him, I'm letting him off the hook. I want to punish him by not forgiving.

_____ I have a right to be angry.

_____ Other_____

I've been guilty of some of these thoughts. If you have been, too, perhaps it's because we don't really understand how much it cost Jesus to forgive us. *"But God demonstrates his own love for us in this: While we were still sinners, Christ died for us"* (Romans 5:8). If Jesus sacrificed His life and forgave us of so much, shouldn't we forgive the smaller offenses of others?

Forgiveness is needed in relationships between people of all ages. When my grade-school-aged grandsons came over, one brother became angry with the other and refused to forgive. This provided an opportunity to discuss forgiveness. To help my grandson not hold a grudge, I said, "I suppose if Grandpa does something I don't like, I should stay mad at him." I continued, "I won't talk to him or do anything for him. Would that work?"

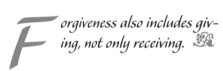

orgiveness also includes giving, not only receiving.

My grandson remained silent for a while, and I wondered if he understood what I had said. Before long he replied, "Okay, I'll forgive him."

In Luke 7:36–50, Jesus used an illustration to teach about

forgiveness. Let's read the true story as a play with a cast of three main characters: Jesus, Simon the Pharisee, and a woman. You'll find a story within the story.

5. As you read the passage in script form, read Simon's part aloud, and listen to Jesus' words of response.

NARRATOR: Now one of the Pharisees invited Jesus to have dinner with him, so he went to the Pharisee's house and reclined at the table. When a woman who had lived a sinful life in that town learned that Jesus was eating at the Pharisee's house, she brought an alabaster jar of perfume, and as she stood behind him at his feet weeping, she began to wet his feet with her tears. Then she wiped them with her hair, kissed them and poured perfume on them.

SIMON *(to himself): If this man were a prophet, he would know who is touching him and what kind of woman she is—that she is a sinner.*

JESUS: Simon, I have something to tell you.

SIMON: Tell me, teacher.

JESUS: Two men owed money to a certain money-lender. One owed him five hundred denarii, and the other fifty. Neither of them had the money to pay him back, so he canceled the debts of both. Now which of them will love him more?

SIMON: I suppose the one who had the bigger debt canceled.

JESUS: You have judged correctly. *[Turning toward the WOMAN and speaking to SIMON]* Do you see this woman? I came into your house. You did not give me any water for my feet, but she wet my feet with her tears and wiped them with her hair. You did not give me a kiss, but this woman, from the time I entered, has not stopped kissing my feet. You did not put oil on my head, but she has poured perfume on my feet. Therefore, I tell you, her many sins have been forgiven—for she loved much. But he who has been forgiven little loves little. [To the WOMAN] Your sins are forgiven.

OTHER GUESTS (among themselves): Who is this who even forgives sins?

JESUS (to the woman): Your faith has saved you; go in peace.

6. Who is the hero or heroine of the story?

_____

Who is the villain?

_____

7. Which character do you identify with most? Why?

_____

_____

_____

_____

8. What is Simon's response to Jesus?

_____

_____

_____

To the woman?

_____

_____

_____

In this passage, it appears Simon judges not only the woman but Jesus as well. In Luke 6:37 Jesus says, *"Do not judge, and you will not be judged. Do not condemn, and you will not be condemned. Forgive, and you will be forgiven."*

From this story, we see God doesn't condone sin *or* condemn the sinner. Instead, He forgives those who repent.

In our relationships, forgiveness doesn't mean we excuse and accept the wrong behavior of others. Nor do we condemn people. In situations beyond our control, we pray and leave the outcome to God. Forgiveness is not a one-time action; it's ongoing.

> Forgive whatever grievances you may have against one another. Forgive as the Lord forgave you. (Colossians 3:13)

Sometimes the process of forgiveness feels like a tug of war. God tugs at our hearts to forgive, but we hang on to unforgiveness and keep pulling on our end of the rope. However, if we let go, the rope goes slack, and God helps us forgive. Even though it seems as if we've lost the tug of war, we've actually won.

9. In your grandparenting relationships, is there someone you're angry with or holding a grudge against? Is there someone you need to forgive? If so, ask God to help you forgive that person. Or do you need to ask someone to forgive you? Write your prayer here:

_____

_____

_____

_____

_____

_____

GRAND Thought: Forgiveness is a gift we give ourselves. When we forgive others, we're not only obeying God, but we are also released from the bondage of unforgiveness.

Prayer: Lord Jesus, thank You for dying for my sins and forgiving me. While I was a sinner, even before I had any interest in You, You died for me. Help me to be more like You so I love and forgive others. I can't do it on my own, but with Your help I can. I don't want to hold grudges toward others. Thank You for helping me forgive.

(Based on Romans 5:8)

Weekend Devotion

Sacrificial Love

You see, at just the right time, when we were still powerless, Christ died for the ungodly. (Romans 5:6)

📖 Read: Romans 5:1–11

"How are you doing?" I asked my pregnant daughter when she called after her seven-month checkup.

"Okay, I guess." Her voice sounded flat. I could tell something was wrong. She paused. "The doctor put me on bed rest so the baby won't come too early."

I sighed. That wasn't what I wanted to hear. We had prayed she would get through this pregnancy without the complications of her last one. With two-year-old Peter to care for, how could she rest? Although I had barely recovered from a lengthy illness with high fevers and hospitalization, I wanted to help her. After all, she's my daughter and I love her.

So I made the hour-long drive to her home several days a week to help with meals, housework, and caring for Peter. My home chores remained undone while I completed hers. One day as I left her home, I said, "I'm investing in the life of my unborn grandson. Otherwise, he might not have a life."

Later, I realized Christ did the same for us. He invested in our lives before we were born or born again so we could have abundant life. But more importantly, so we could have *eternal* life. *"You see, at just the right time, when we were still powerless, Christ died for the ungodly"* (v. 6). Why did He die for us? To demonstrate His love (v. 8).

I made a small sacrifice of time and energy to help my daughter during her weeks on bed rest. As a result, she gave birth to a healthy son, our second grandchild, Alex. But Jesus made the supreme sacrifice by giving His life so we might live.

Prayer: Thank You, Lord, for Your wonderful, sacrificial love. While I was an undeserving sinner, You died for me. Help me demonstrate Your self-giving love to others, especially my grandchildren.

Prepare to Pray

(God answers knee-mail)

When I asked Grandma Elaine what practical advice she would give soon-to-be grandparents, she replied: "PRAY! Pray over big decisions and challenges. Pray over little stuff. Let them hear you praying for them regularly."

Grandma Elaine doesn't just talk about prayer. She meets weekly with other grandmothers to pray for their grandchildren.

Just as my grandkids like to open the toy tool chest and pretend to fix things with the hammer and saw, we'll focus on important tools of prayer. But these aren't pretend. They really work! God has the power to fix our problems, and He wants us to call on Him. So let's take our power tools and ask God to impact our grandchildren's lives through prayer. Together we'll learn:

Day One	When to Pray
Day Two	How to Pray
Day Three	What to Pray
Day Four	Why Pray?
Day Five	How to Teach Grandchildren to Pray

When to Pray

When Grandma Gail learned she would become a grandmother, she wrote, "We are expecting our first grandchild! We are thrilled and already praying for this little life as God's knitting needles go to work!"

Heartwork

If you knit or have watched someone knit, you know that all the yarn passes through the knitter's hands before it becomes part of the item created. That's why I love the picture of God's work on our unborn grandchildren in Psalm 139:

> *13For you created my inmost being; you knit me together in my mother's womb. 14I praise you because I am fearfully and wonderfully made; your works are wonderful, I know that full well. 15My frame was not hidden from you when I was made in the secret place. When I was woven together in the depths of the earth, 16your eyes saw my unformed body. All the days ordained for me were written in your book before one of them came to be.* (Psalm 139:13–16)

1. In the verses above, we see God's active involvement in forming our grandchildren. Circle the verbs that show how God formed them.

2. How does this passage describe the quality of God's workmanship?

_____

_____

3. How do you see God's workmanship reflected in your grandchildren? Record your thoughts.

_____

_____

_____

According to Psalm 139:15, our grandchildren are formed in secret. Nowadays, with ultrasounds, we may see a glimpse of our grandchild in the womb. But our omniscient (all-knowing) God doesn't need an ultrasound—they are not hidden from Him.

4. Even before our grandchildren were born, what did God know about them according to Psalm 139:15, 16 (above) and Jeremiah 1:5?

> *"Before I formed you in the womb I knew you, before you were born I set you apart."*

_____

If God is so intimately involved in forming our grandchildren in the womb, shouldn't we pray for them before their birth? Grandma Erna said, "I asked God to guard and protect the embryo as it developed each day." Now she delights in God's answer—a healthy grandson (who is, of course, above average in her viewpoint).

When our daughter Anita told us they were expecting a baby, my husband, Grandpa Milt, immediately added this unborn child to his daily prayer list. As my husband and I prayed together that night, he said, "May this child become Your child, not just ours."

Our daughter recorded Grandpa Milt's prayer next to the scrapbooked photo of her newborn. She also added, "How blessed to have a praying grandpa." God answered Milt's prayer, and Peter accepted Christ as his Savior at an early age.

Is your grandchild blessed with a praying grandparent? It's never too soon to begin praying for your future grandchildren. I know grandparents who began praying for their grandchildren when their children married. Others began even sooner—when their own children were born. I pray our current grandchildren and all generations born from now until Christ's return will follow God with wholehearted devotion.

Not only are we encouraged to pray before their birth, but the Bible also offers specific instructions on when to pray after our grandchildren arrive.

5. The apostle Paul, in 1 Thessalonians 5:17 writes, *"Pray continually."* What does that mean to you?

_____

_____

Other versions say it this way:

> *Pray without ceasing.* (KJV)
> *Pray all the time.* (MSG)
> *Never stop praying.* (NLT)

No matter what Bible version you read, none says, "Pray if you feel like it" or, "Pray occasionally."

Obviously, we can't go around with our heads bowed and pray while driving, while at work, or sleeping. But we can remain in a constant attitude of prayer and praise. We can also depend on God and call on Him throughout the day. My pastor explained that praying should be as automatic as breathing. When we see God provide for us, or work in our lives, we immediately say, "Thank you, Lord." When we have a need, we pray for help. When the Holy Spirit shows us a sinful attitude, we immediately confess it and ask God to help us overcome our sin.

With our grandchildren, our prayers should be spontaneous, too. When little ones fall and hurt themselves, we can gather them into our arms, comfort them, and pray aloud that God would soothe them. "Oh, Lord, please touch Alex's owie and help him feel better." When older grandchildren share a concern, or we sense

We need to weave prayer into our everyday lives.

they are struggling, we can pray *for* them and *with* them. When one grandmother of a preteen learned her granddaughter was having a tough time in Social Studies, she asked her granddaughter the time of that class and promised to pray for her then. This comforted her granddaughter and made a difference.

Paul also encourages us to pray in another of his epistles: "Devote *yourselves to prayer, being watchful and thankful*" (Colossians 4:2, emphasis added).

6. What are you dedicated or consecrated to? How do you spend your time and energy? In prayer? If not, write a prayer below, asking God to make you a praying grandparent.

_____

_____

_____

_____

When our four-year-old granddaughter was about to perform in a ballet, I went backstage to see the cute little bumblebee before she danced. She seemed excited and nervous. In the hubbub of other dancers, we hugged and I prayed aloud that she would do a good job and not be afraid. After I said, "Amen," she added in a loud voice, "AMEN!" What a sweet moment we shared! And, although I do have a grandmotherly bias, the sixty-second flight of this bumblebee was fantastic!

When was the last time you prayed with your grandchildren or for them?

As we read in Psalm 139:16, *"All the days ordained for me were written in your book before one of them came to be."* Do you wonder what it says about you on the pages of that book? I want my pages to say, "She prayed for her grandchildren."

> From birth I have relied on you; you brought me forth from my mother's womb. I will ever praise you. (Psalm 71:6)

Remember, it's never too early or too late to begin praying for our grandchildren.

GRAND Thought: Even *before* our grandchildren cut their teeth, let's cut our teeth on prayer.

Prayer: Heavenly Father, thank You for the privilege of praying for my precious grandchildren. You already know all about them because You knit them together according to Your plans. Make me a faithful prayer warrior, often bringing my grandchildren to You. Prompt my heart to pray continually. May I devote myself to praying for my grandchildren.

Day Two

How to Pray

"Who will pray for me now?" our teenage son Jonathan asked when he lost both grandparents within months.

His question startled me. He knew my husband and I prayed for him every day. But he also knew that my parents had prayed aloud for him daily for sixteen years. If Jonathan had a French horn competition or challenging tests, they prayed—and he felt their prayers in God's answers. Now he sensed a loss, missing his grandparents and their prayer support. He wondered, *Will I be as successful without their prayers?* Indeed, who *would* pray for him now?

His question prompted me to join a Moms In Touch prayer group (www.momsintouch.org). Perhaps our group's united prayers could replace his grandparents' powerful prayers. I also tucked my son's question away in my heart, knowing someday I might have grandchildren who would need my prayers.

Now, my husband and I pray for our grandchildren daily. I also pray for them weekly with other grandmothers. Our prayer group uses the four-step format I learned in Moms In

Touch: praise, silent confession, thanksgiving, and intercession. Perhaps you've heard of a similar format with the acrostic ACTS (adoration, confession, thanksgiving, and supplication).

Before I joined this group, my prayers often consisted of bringing my long list of requests to God. Perhaps I treated God like a magic genie: Rub, ask for three wishes, requests granted. But learning this new prayer format transformed my prayer life. Whether you're taking your first wobbly baby steps in prayer, or have been skipping along with confidence for years, these four steps will strengthen your prayer life and bless your grandchildren.

Heartwork

Step One: Praise God

Praising God means focusing on Him and who He is. When we praise Him, we're not praying for others or ourselves; we're thinking about God and His attributes. Is He loving? Is He trustworthy? Yes, of course. That's what we tell Him as we praise Him for *who* He is, not what He does in answer to our prayers.

It's easier for me to understand praising God when I compare it to my relationships with my grandchildren. When they were babies, they smiled and gurgled and sometimes slobbered on me to express their love. Now older, they give me hugs and kisses and say, "I love you."

When we praise God, we're drawing close to Him and telling Him, "I love You. You're wonderful. You're trustworthy." Just as we smile when our grandkids compliment us or hug us, God smiles when we praise Him. The book of Psalms ends, *"Let everything that has breath praise the LORD. Praise the LORD"* (Psalm 150:6).

Using a Scripture passage or a worship song helps me focus on God's specific attributes and give Him praise. The Bible is full of passages that express praise to God. Today we'll look at Psalm 23 and find reasons to praise Him.

1. Underline the words that reveal aspects of God's character, or who He is.

The LORD is my shepherd, I shall not be in want. He makes me lie down in green pastures, he leads me beside quiet waters, he restores my soul. He guides me in paths of righteousness for his name's sake. Even though I walk through the valley of the shadow of death, I will fear no evil, for you are with me; your rod and your staff, they comfort me. You prepare a table before me in the presence of my enemies. You anoint my head with oil; my cup overflows. Surely goodness and love will follow me all the days of my life, and I will dwell in the house of the LORD forever.

2. Now write a simple prayer, praising God for these attributes. You could start by saying, "Lord, I praise You because . . . (e.g., You are my shepherd and provide everything I need).

_____

_____

_____

_____

> I call to the Lord, who is worthy of praise. (Psalm 18:3)

Although I joined a Moms In Touch group to request things for my children, now my favorite part of our grandmothers' prayer time is praising God.

Step Two: Confess Sins

During this time we ask God to search our hearts and forgive any sins He reveals. It's a time to let God scrub us clean. In a prayer group, confession is usually done silently.

When my grandkids do something wrong, I'm pleased when they admit their mistakes and apologize. Similarly, when we fail, God wants to hear our prayer of repentance.

> Search me, O God, and know my heart; test me and know my anxious thoughts. See if there is any offensive way in me, and lead me in the way everlasting. (Psalm 139:23, 24)

3. Psalm 66:18 gives us a good reason to repent. What is it?

If I had cherished sin in my heart, the Lord would not have listened.

_____

_____

_____

4. Based on 1 John 1:9, what will God do if we confess our sins?

If we confess our sins, he is faithful and just and will forgive us our sins and purify us from all unrighteousness.

_____

_____

_____

In the Bible, we read that King David committed adultery and murder. But when he cried out and confessed his sin, God forgave him.

Have mercy on me, O God, according to your unfailing love; according to your great compassion blot out my transgressions. Wash away all my iniquity and cleanse me from my sin. For I know my transgressions, and my sin is always before me. . . . Cleanse me with hyssop, and I will be clean; wash me, and I will be whiter than snow. . . . Create in me a pure heart, O God, and renew a steadfast spirit within me. (Psalm 51:1–3, 7, 10)

5. Ask God, "Is there anything I need to confess?" If so, pray David's prayer of confession, or write your own prayer.

_____

_____

_____

Remember—when we confess, God forgives. It's as if we've written our sins on a child's magic slate. Then God lifts the sheet and erases our sins. Right then, we can begin again with a clean slate.

> As far as the east is from the west, so far has he removed our transgressions from us.
> (Psalm 103:12)

Step Three: Thank God

Next we thank God for answered prayers. *"Enter his gates with thanksgiving and his courts with praise; give thanks to him and praise his name. For the LORD is good"* (Psalm 100:4, 5).

I love to hear my grandkids thank me when I do things for them. Four-year-old Owen often asks for a plain flour tortilla, one of his favorite foods. When I give it to him, he sweetly says, "Thank you." His response makes my heart smile, and I wonder what else I can do for him.

God loves to hear *us* say thank you, too. Remember the story in Luke 17:11–19 about Jesus healing the ten lepers? Sadly, only one returned to thank Him. Can't you hear the disappointment in Jesus' voice when he asked, "Were not all ten cleansed? Where are the other nine?" (v. 17).

I don't want to be like the nine lepers who didn't return to say thanks. But often I am. When God answers my prayer, I forget to thank Him, and sometimes I don't even remember what I prayed for!

One way to remember God's faithfulness is to record your prayers and God's answers in a journal. Perhaps you'd like to make a grandparents' prayer journal to list your prayers and God's answers. Use any style notebook and add columns for requests, how God answered, and the dates of both. You could also add a picture of your grandchild in your journal. Or if you have several grandchildren, make a separate section for each one. For those with dozens of grandkids, ask God for creative ways to organize your prayers for them. Perhaps a recipe file with dividers would work.

Great-Grandma Bobbi keeps track of praying for her three children, eight grandchildren, and fifteen great-grandchildren this way: "I pray for them by family. I start with my oldest child and pray for his children and grandchildren. I pray for each one by name every day."

6. What can we learn about God's view of thanksgiving from Psalm 50:23?

He who offers a sacrifice of thanksgiving honors Me. (NASB)

_____

_____

_____

_____

7. How has God answered some of your recent prayer requests for your grandchildren? List them and thank God for

the answers. If you don't remember recent answers, thank God for things you like about your grandchildren: sweet attitudes, cute dimples, or their love for Jesus.

_____

_____

_____

_____

_____

When I recall what God has done and thank Him, it lifts my spirit. Thanksgiving is more than a season of the year. God smiles when our lives reflect *thanks-living* throughout the year.

Step Four: Intercede for Grandchildren

Now we bring our concerns and requests to God.

If my grandchildren have a problem while they're staying with me, I hope they'll come to me with it. Because I love them, I want to help. In the same way, God is concerned about whatever concerns you, His child. Nothing is too big or too small to pray about. *"You can throw the whole weight of your anxieties upon him, for you are his personal concern"* (1 Peter 5:7, Phillips).

> **And pray in the Spirit on all occasions with all kinds of prayers and requests. With this in mind, be alert and always keep on praying for all the saints. (Ephesians 6:18)**

8. List several requests for your grandchildren. If you have a prayer journal, write them there. Then talk to God about your concerns, and pray for His will in their lives.

_____

_____

_____

_____

_____

Our next lesson will cover a powerful way to pray for our grandchildren using Scripture.

9. Read Ephesians 3:20, 21 in *The Message* to learn what God can do through your prayers:

> *If you aren't praying for your grandchild, who is?*

God can do anything, you know—far more than you could ever imagine or guess or request in your wildest dreams! He does it not by pushing us around but by working within us, his Spirit deeply and gently within us.
Glory to God in the church!
Glory to God in the Messiah, in Jesus!
Glory down all the generations!
Glory through all millennia! Oh, yes!

These verses motivate me to pray!

Remember, you are praying to an infinite God, whose resources are infinite. *"For nothing is impossible with God"* (Luke 1:37).

Now that we've covered the four steps of prayer, let's get started praying. At first, this new format might feel stiff, like a new pair of shoes. That's okay. It felt uncomfortable for me, too. But shoes stretch and mold to our feet, and in time they feel comfortable and natural. So take the first step. As you use this format and praise God, confess sin, give thanks, and intercede, before long, you'll be striding along in prayer.

10. Personal: How would you describe your prayer life? In what way(s) would you like it to change? Write a prayer, asking God to help you grow in your communication with Him.

_____

_____

_____

_____

GRAND Thought: When I praise and thank God, it changes my perspective on my problems. And when I confess my sin, it opens the channel for God to hear and answer my prayers.

Prayer: Dear Lord, I praise You as my Shepherd—yes, *my* Shepherd. You want to lead me and guide me in paths of righteousness and beside quiet waters. And I want to follow. Forgive me for the times I haven't, and thank You for Your forgiveness, goodness, and mercy. Now, Lord, take hold of me in new ways. Set me apart for You and use me in the lives of my precious grandchildren.

Praise + confession + thanksgiving + intercession = prayer power!

What to Pray

During his morning devotions, my husband, Grandpa Milt, reads his Bible and notes verses that apply to our family. Then he uses the verses as the basis for his prayers. As he daily kneels and prays from God's Word for each grandchild, he makes an eternal impact on their lives! Seeing my husband in prayer is the dearest sight for me. After years of praying this way, he has stacks of notebooks filled with verses he has prayed. Praying from Scripture is a powerful way to influence our grandchildren's lives.

Heartwork

Praying for our grandchildren is serious business.

1. As you read Lamentations 2:19, underline the words that express the urgency behind Jeremiah's words.

> *Arise, cry out in the night, as the watches of the night begin; pour out your heart like water in the presence of the Lord. Lift up your hands to him for the lives of your children.*

What's going on in this passage? It was the year 586 BC, and the Babylonian army had destroyed the city of Jerusalem. Jeremiah saw the smoldering city and starving children and wrote this lament. In the midst of describing the horrendous things he witnessed, he exhorted the people to pray—to cry out to God for the lives of their children.[1]

When Jeremiah tells them to pray, it's *not*, "If you feel like it and think it might be a good idea, then perhaps you'd like to consider praying for your children once in a while." No! It's *"Wake up* and pray! *Cry out* to God! *Pour out your hearts* to Him!" Prayer is more important than sleeping.

Our circumstances may not be as dire as those in Jerusalem in 586 BC, but let's not wait for unthinkable events to happen before we get serious about praying. Let's put a hedge of protection around our grandchildren *now* through our faithful, consistent prayers.

2. Isaiah 62:6 also emphasizes the importance of calling on God for those we love: *"I have posted watchmen on your walls,*

O Jerusalem; they will never be silent day or night. You who call on the LORD, give yourselves no rest. "

According to this verse, when should we pray?

_____

Every grandchild needs praying grandparents. What a privilege to be watchmen on the wall and protect them through our prayers! Even if we can't be with them, God can touch them through our prayers.

How important do you think it is to pray for your grandchildren? Ask God to help you pray earnestly and *"pour out your heart like water"* to Him for the lives of your grandchildren.

3. Let's look at ways to use Scripture in our prayers for our grandchildren. The chart on pages 46–47 contains an acrostic of the word *grandchild*, with character traits we can pray for our grandchildren. I've included a verse that emphasizes each trait and have written a sample prayer based on the verse. Check three character traits you'd like to see developed in your grandchild.

You could pray daily for one character trait per week. Then move on to the next trait. Or, make your own list of traits and verses to pray. Dick Eastman, author of several prayer books, said, "By bringing God's Word directly into our praying, we are bringing God's power directly into our praying."

Another way to pray from Scripture for your grandchildren is to make an acrostic with your grandchild's name. Select character traits and verses, and pray for your grandchild from your customized list. I've done that for our grandson Peter:

P **Purity:** *Run from anything that stimulates youthful lusts. Instead, pursue righteous living, faithfulness, love, and peace. Enjoy the companionship of those who call on the Lord with pure hearts.* (2 Timothy 2:22 NLT)

E **Endurance:** *I have fought a good fight, I have finished my course, I have kept the faith.* (2 Timothy 4:7 KJV)

T **Teachability:** *My son, if you accept my words and store up my commands within you, . . . wisdom will enter your heart, and knowledge will be pleasant to your soul.* (Proverbs 2:1, 10)

E **Encourages others:** *Therefore encourage one another and build each other up, just as in fact you are doing.* (1 Thessalonians 5:11)

R **Responsibility:** *Each one should use whatever gift he has received to serve others, faithfully administering God's grace in its various forms.* (1 Peter 4:10)

> *The most promising method of prayer is to allow oneself to be guided by the word of the Scriptures. . . . In this way we shall not become the victims of our own emptiness."* Dietrich Bonhoeffer

4. If you want to pray Scripture-based prayers for your current or future grandchildren, select a method that works for you—perhaps using verses in the chart, making an acrostic with your grandchild's name, or another idea. Record your prayer plan here:

_____

_____

_____

Praying Scripture for Your Grandchild

	Character Trait	Bible Verses	Scripture-Based Prayer
G	Gentleness	*Let your gentleness be evident to all.* (Philippians 4:5)	I pray ———— will be known for his/her gentleness.
R	Respect	*Show proper respect to everyone: Love the brotherhood of believers, fear God, honor the king.* (1 Peter 2:17)	I pray ———— will show respect to everyone. May he/she also love other Christians, fear God, and honor those in authority.
A	Availability	*"Whom shall I send? And who will go for us?" And I said, "Here am I. Send me!"* (Isaiah 6:8)	I pray that whenever ———— hears Your call, he/she will gladly respond, "Here am I, send me!"
N	Nonconformity	*Do not conform any longer to the pattern of this world, but be transformed by the renewing of your mind. Then you will be able to test and approve what God's will is—his good, pleasing and perfect will.* (Romans 12:2)	I pray ———— will not conform to the pattern of the world. Instead may he/she be transformed by the renewing of his/her mind so he/she can test and approve God's good, pleasing, and perfect will.
D	Discernment	*And this is my prayer: that your love may abound more and more in knowledge and depth of insight, so that you may be able to discern what is best and may be pure and blameless until the day of Christ.* (Philippians 1:9, 10)	I pray ———— will love God more and more, and will abound in knowledge and insight, so he/she can discern what is best and be pure and blameless until the day of Christ.

C	Courage	*"Be strong and courageous. Do not be terrified; do not be discouraged, for the LORD your God will be with you wherever you go." (Joshua 1:9)*	I pray _____ will be strong and courageous and not be terrified or discouraged. Help _____ realize that You, God, are with him/her wherever he/she goes.
H	Humility	*Humble yourselves before the Lord, and he will lift you up. (James 4:10)*	I pray _____ will humble himself/herself before You, Lord, so You can lift him/her up.
I	Integrity	*May integrity and uprightness protect me, because my hope is in you. (Psalm 25:21)*	I pray _____ will be protected by integrity and uprightness. Help him/her live with integrity and hope in You.
L	Loyalty	*"O LORD, God of our fathers . . . keep their hearts loyal to you. And give my son Solomon the wholehearted devotion to keep your commands, requirements and decrees." (1 Chronicles 29:18, 19)*	Oh, Lord, keep _____'s heart loyal to You. Give him/her wholehearted devotion to keep all Your commands, requirements, and decrees.
D	Diligence	*Be diligent in these matters; give yourself wholly to them, so that everyone may see your progress. (1 Timothy 4:15)*	I pray _____ will be diligent in all he/she does, giving himself/herself wholly to Your work so everyone sees his/her progress.

Another way to use Scripture is to pray about different topics each day of the week, as shown in the chart below. To personalize prayers for your grandchildren, create your own chart with specific topics and Scripture passages.

Day	Prayer Topic	Scripture
Sunday	Salvation and spiritual growth	*"Open their eyes and turn them from darkness to light, and from the power of Satan to God, so that they may receive forgiveness of sins and a place among those who are sanctified by faith in me." (Acts 26:18)*
Monday	Obedience to God's Word	*Keep my commands and you will live; guard my teachings as the apple of your eye. Bind them on your fingers; write them on the tablet of your heart. (Proverbs 7:2, 3)*
Tuesday	Strong, loving family relationships	*Be devoted to one another in brotherly love. Honor one another above yourselves. (Romans 12:10)*
Wednesday	Faithful, godly friends (including future mate)	*If one falls down, his friend can help him up. But pity the man who falls and has no one to help him up! (Ecclesiastes 4:10)*
Thursday	Recognition and development of God-given talents; future career	*I have filled him with the Spirit of God, with skill, ability and knowledge in all kinds of crafts. (Exodus 31:3)*
Friday	Good health and God's protection	*He will cover you with his feathers, and under his wings you will find refuge; . . . For he will command his angels concerning you to guard you in all your ways. (Psalm 91:4, 11)*
Saturday	Teachability; others who impact their lives: Sunday school teachers, school teachers, coaches, etc.	*"Now then, my sons, listen to me; blessed are those who keep my ways."* (Proverbs 8:32)

Chart inspired from "Praying for Your Children" by Jeanne Zornes, *LIVE,* (May 4, 2008).

5. One of Satan's tricks is to keep us too busy to pray. Don't let him succeed. What steps can you take, starting today, to schedule powerful prayer times for your grandchildren?

_____

_____

_____

_____

6. Write a prayer for your grandchild. Pray it for several days, then consider sending a copy of the prayer to your grandchild.

_____

_____

_____

_____

_____

_____

> *When a Christian shuns fellowship with other Christians, the devil smiles. When he stops studying the Bible, the devil laughs. When he stops praying, the devil shouts for joy."*
> *Corrie ten Boom*

We can talk about prayer and praying, but there's no power in talking. We can read about prayer and learn different methods to pray, but there's no power in reading. The power comes when we connect with God Almighty *and pray.*

The bottom line of this lesson is: PRAY! Cry out to God as if your prayers make a difference—*because they do.*

GRAND Thought: God works through our prayers. If we pray, we will change the course of our grandchildren's futures for good.

Prayer: Lord, You have a hope and a future for each of my grandchildren. I want to cooperate with Your plan by faithfully praying for them. May it be true about me that I have not stopped praying for my grandchildren and asking You to fill them with the knowledge of Your will through all spiritual wisdom and understanding. I also pray that my grandchildren will be like Jesus, growing *"in wisdom and stature, and in favor with God and men,"* so they become well-rounded individuals. I pray they will grow intellectually, physically, spiritually, and relationally. Thank You for your deep love for them and me.

(Based on Jeremiah 29:11; Colossians 1:9; Luke 2:52)

If your grandchild asked you, "Why do you pray?" how would you answer?

I might say, "I'm God's child, and He likes to hear from me," or, "God hears my prayers and helps me," or, "God has power, and I don't."

There are many reasons why people pray. Let's look at three biblical reasons to do so. Whether the passages are new or familiar, I pray God will give you fresh insights on why to pray.

Heartwork

A Gift to God

In Revelation, the final book of the Bible, the apostle John writes that a door to heaven opened and a voice called, *"Come up here"* (Revelation 4:1). Then John describes his vision of things to come. The "He" in this passage refers to the Lamb of God.

> *He came and took the scroll from the right hand of him who sat on the throne. And when he had taken it, the four living creatures and the twenty-four elders fell down before the Lamb. Each one had a harp and they were holding golden bowls full of incense, which are the prayers of the saints.* (Revelation 5:7, 8)

Picture this breathtaking, holy scene: God sits on the throne. The Lamb of God (the risen Jesus) takes the scroll. And four living creatures and twenty-four elders bow in worship.

1. Circle the two things the living creatures and elders bring with them to use in worship.

2. Using harps in worship may not be surprising. But what do the golden bowls contain?

_____

3. What does this indicate about the value of our prayers? (e.g., do you save things you treasure?)

_____

_____

4. In Revelation 8:3, 4, John continues with his glimpse into heaven. Now he sees an angel before an altar. Circle what the angel offers.

> *Another angel, who had a golden censer, came and stood at the altar. He was given much incense to offer, with the prayers of all the saints, on the golden altar before the throne. The smoke of the incense, together with the prayers of the saints, went up before God from the angel's hand.*

Picture what John sees: An angel stands before a holy God to offer something precious. And your prayers and mine are part of the offering. Does it surprise you that God values our prayers? That He accumulates them in golden bowls, and they are a fragrant offering of incense to Him? I wept when I realized how precious my simple, often faltering prayers are to a holy, omnipotent God. I pray the enormity of this thought will grip your heart, too.

In Psalm 141:2, David also speaks of our prayers as incense: *"May my prayer be set before you like incense; may the lifting up of my hands be like the evening sacrifice."*

How precious to know our prayers are a gift of worship to God! They rise up to Him, and He treasures them.

Choose an attractive bowl and set it where you study your Bible and pray. Write your prayers of praise or requests on slips of paper. Place them in the bowl as an act of worship to God. Include a prayer to thank God that your prayers matter to Him.

5. Read 1 Peter 3:12 to learn more about how God values our prayers: *"For the eyes of the Lord are on the righteous and his ears are attentive to their prayer."*

Of our five senses, which two are mentioned in this verse?

Picture your grandchild running to you with a request. If you're not busy, you're eager to listen. Sometimes when my granddaughter wants to talk to me or show me a picture she colored, I'm too busy to give her my full attention. She may tug on my arm and say, "Grandma, Grandma," until I stop what I'm doing, look at her, and really listen.

But God is *never* too busy. He values our prayers and doesn't haphazardly listen when we pray. His ears are attentive. We get His full attention. Other Bible versions of 1 Peter 3:12 say it this way:

> *God looks on all this with approval, listening and responding well to what he's asked.* (MSG)

> *The eyes of the Lord watch over those who do right, and his ears are open to their prayers.* (NLT)

God is "all ears" when it comes to our prayers. We are God's children, and He loves to hear from His kids even more than we enjoy hearing from our grandkids. Recently when Clara and I talked on the phone, she ended our chat with, "I love you, Grandma." What a delight to my heart! Our prayers delight God, too. They are a gift to Him. He gathers them in bowls because they are precious.

Now let's look at the second reason to pray.

A Gift to You

Let's learn why prayer is a gift to you. James 4:8 (NASB) says: *"Draw near to God and He will draw near to you."*

6. What would it look like for you to draw near to God? How could you put that into a picture? Try drawing it here, or express your thoughts in words.

What happens when we draw near to God?

_____

_____

As we draw near to God, our relationship with Him grows, and we are blessed through sweet communion.

7. Hebrews 4:16 also speaks about approaching God. Underline the words that say how we are to come to Him.

> The LORD is near to all who call on him. (Psalm 145:18)

> _Let us then approach the throne of grace with confidence, so that we may receive mercy and find grace to help us in our time of need._

What is the result of coming to God?

_____

_____

This verse also mentions _when_ to come: _"in our time of need."_ Do you have needs? List them below, or write them on slips of paper and add them to your "golden bowl of incense" for the Lord.

_____

_____

_____

What a joy to realize our prayers not only delight God, they also draw us closer to Him. Now let's consider the third reason to pray.

A Gift to Our Grandchildren

As grandparents, we hate to see our grandkids suffer. And when they do, we'd like to "kiss them and make it all better." But many concerns are beyond our control and can't be kissed away. Although we want to _do_ something, often there is nothing we _can_ do. In the past, I would say in a sad, defeated voice, "All I can do is pray," as if my prayers didn't amount to much. But I've learned prayer is not a small, insignificant _all_. Prayer is a huge ALL, because I'm praying to the One who is All in all, and He has all power.

> Of all the gifts we can give our grandchildren, prayer is the best.

Remember playing "so big" with your grandkids? You'd say, "How big is _____ ?" and they would raise their arms and say, "So big." With God, we need to remind ourselves and teach our grandchildren that God is S-O-O-O-O-O BIG as we raise our arms above our heads and point upward.

8. Read James 5:16 and underline the impact of our prayers because God is all-powerful.

> *The prayer of a righteous man is powerful and effective.*

> *The earnest prayer of a righteous person has great power and produces wonderful results.* (NLT)

> *The effective prayer of a righteous man can accomplish much.* (NASB)

As exciting as James 5:16 is, do you know the context of this familiar verse? These two verses follow verse 16:

> *Elijah was a man just like us. He prayed earnestly that it would not rain, and it did not rain on the land for three and a half years. Again he prayed, and the heavens gave rain, and the earth produced its crops.*

9. Underline the words that tell what kind of man Elijah was.

If God started and stopped a drought based on the prayers of an ordinary man, what might He do through *your* prayers?

Even though we may not see all our prayers answered in our lifetime, remember that God saves them and may answer them after we're gone.

Great-Grandmother Bobbi said, "I pray for my children, grandchildren, and great-grandchildren every day. Some of them aren't Christians, and I pray for their salvation. I tell Satan, 'You can't have any of them. They belong to God!' And I daily claim their salvation. Since I'm in my eighties, I may not see them become Christians in my lifetime, but I believe God will save them all."

Do Bobbi's prayers make a difference in her grandchildren's and great-grandchildren's lives? Who would deny that? Her prayers are an eternal gift to them.

> **Nothing is too hard for you.**
> **(Jeremiah 32:17)**
>
> **"With God all things are possible." (Matthew 19:26)**

Since we know why to pray, why don't we? When a large church polled its members and asked, "Why don't people pray?" some answered, "I don't know how," or "I don't understand prayer." Are these good excuses? Don't we do other things we don't know about or understand, like flying in airplanes or using electricity? If we're interested, we can learn how. Maybe we aren't motivated or don't understand the importance of prayer.

Our pastor suggested these possible reasons why we don't pray:

1. We don't know what we're missing.
2. We have bought the lie that other things are more important.
3. The powers of darkness make sure we don't pray because our prayers are a threat to the enemy.[2]

To illustrate the first reason, here's a humorous story Grandpa Bill told about his grandson:

When Jeff came home from preschool, his mother asked, "Did you have a nice day?"

"No," Jeff replied. "I knocked Massey down, and I feel so bad."

"Let's pray about it," his mother said.

"Oh, no, don't tell God," Jeff said. "Then I'll really be in trouble."

We chuckle at this story. Like Jeff, maybe we don't understand prayer or don't know what we're missing by not praying. Perhaps we're afraid God will be angry if we make mistakes. We don't realize how much He loves us and wants us to come to Him with every concern.

People also think other things are more important than prayer. It's the tyranny of the urgent—letting immediate things crowd out what is most important. Often we have wrong priorities, and the good we do becomes the enemy of the best God has planned for us.

The third reason we don't pray is that the enemy makes sure we don't. William Cowper, who wrote poems and hymns in the 1700s, said, "Satan trembles when he sees the weakest saint upon his knees." The devil would rather see us busy even with good things than tapping into prayer, the believer's source of power.

What about you? How can you make your prayer life more effective? Consider this idea.

Do you have a GPS (Global Positioning System) device in your car to help you find your way? Whether you do or don't, why not establish your own GPS: **G**randparents' **P**rayer **S**ignal? What can you use to guide and direct you to pray?

For example, when I see the transparent plastic teapot my grandson made for my kitchen window, I pray that the light of Jesus will shine through my grandchildren. If you have a GPS in your car, use it as a reminder to pray your grandchildren will follow God's leading and not stray. We can use situations and things around us to prompt us to pray.

10. What can you use as your GPS? List some prayer prompts here:

1. _____
2. _____
3. _____
4. _____
5. _____

Like Daniel in the Bible, it's important to plan specific times to pray. We can schedule prayer first, then fit in other things. If we do other things first, then the important work of prayer is often neglected, which makes the devil jump with glee. We aren't praying, so he doesn't need to worry about the *"powerful and effective"* things God will do through our prayers (James 5:16). Don't let Satan win. Put prayer at the top of your to-do list.

Decide on a specific time and place to pray for your grandchildren daily:

Time: _____
Place: _____

GRAND Thought: Like a grandparent who says, "Come to Grandpa," and welcomes a grandchild into his arms, God calls us to come to Him. He says, "Dear child, run to your Father. I'm calling your name and I long to spend time with you."[3]

Prayer: Heavenly Father, You've touched my heart through Your Word. Thank You for the gift of prayer. I feel loved and affirmed to know You treasure my prayers and save them in a golden bowl. And I'm grateful that when I draw near to You, You draw near to me. You want an intimate, growing relationship with me. And how wonderful to run to You with all my concerns, not only for myself, but also for my grandchildren. You're my loving heavenly Father, and I want to rest in Your embrace.

How to Teach Grandchildren to Pray

Day Five

You may not realize it, but you're teaching your grandkids about prayer. Here's an example from Grandma Cheryl:

> My husband and I took several of our grandchildren on a summer outing to Leavenworth, Washington. Each morning, I took my Bible and coffee and found a quiet corner in the hotel to spend time with God. On the second day, I mentioned to my grandchildren that I read my Bible and pray first thing each morning. The third morning, as I read my Bible, our fourteen-year-old grandson brought his Bible and sat near me. What a blessing! I thanked God my grandson had packed his Bible and wanted to join me.

> *Even when we don't say a word, our actions speak volumes to our grandchildren.*

In today's important lesson, we'll discover how prayer is both caught and taught. Cheryl's experience gives us a personal example of how prayer is caught. Now let's look at a biblical example.

Prayer Is Caught

Perhaps the most familiar Bible passage about prayer is the Lord's Prayer, found in Matthew 6:9–13 (also in Luke 11:2-4). Although I memorized this prayer as a child and recited it at church services, I didn't notice the verse preceding it.

> *One day Jesus was praying in a certain place. When he finished, one of his disciples said to him, "Lord, teach us to pray, just as John taught his disciples." (Luke 11:1)*

1. What was Jesus doing right before one of his disciples asked, "Lord, teach us to pray"?

_____

2. How did Jesus' example influence the disciple's desire to pray?

_____

_____

Was the desire to pray *caught* before prayer was *taught*?
3. As grandparents, what can we learn from Jesus' example?

_____

_____

_____

Our values about prayer make a strong impression on our grandchildren. When two-year-old Peter stayed overnight, he crawled into bed with us and seemed very interested in our nightly conversational prayer. As my husband and I took turns praying, Peter looked back and forth at us, expecting the next one to pray when the other paused. A few times he chimed in with a few words. Peter experienced conversational prayer with us.

I want my grandchildren to learn positive aspects of prayer as they watch me. I'd like to say to them what the apostle Paul said to the Corinthian church in 1 Corinthians 11:1: "Follow my example, as I follow the example of Christ." But to be honest, I'm not always a good role model. So I'd rather tell them, "Follow Christ, not me." However, Jesus isn't walking around on Earth, so *I'm* the one they see.

I've written a prayer to express my desire to set a good example. If it expresses your heart's desire, please pray it with me.

Prayer: Lord Jesus, I'm sorry for the times I've followed my own desires instead of Yours. I repent and ask for help to obey and imitate You. I want to set a worthy example for my grandchildren to follow. When they look at me, I want them to see Jesus in me. Please help me follow You more closely so I can say to my grandchildren without reservation, "Follow Grandma, just as I follow Jesus."

(Based on 1 Corinthians 11:1)

Prayer Is Taught

Besides modeling prayer for our grandchildren, we can also purposely provide opportunities that help them grow in faith and learn to pray.

When my husband lived in Idaho as a young child, he visited his grandparents in Spokane, Washington, during the summers. Although Milt didn't regularly attend church, his grandparents took him to Vacation Bible School (VBS) at their church. The seeds of faith planted in his childhood bore fruit later, and, during his college years, Milt invited Jesus into his life. He still has fond memories of his time with Grandpa and Grandma Perkins, and recently we traveled to Spokane to visit the church where he attended VBS.

Now, we follow his grandparents' example, and our grade-school-aged grandsons stay with us for a week during the summer to attend VBS.

Deuteronomy 6:6–9 offers tips on how and when to pass on our values and faith in the routines of life. Although this passage is written to parents, many grandparents are raising their grandchildren, carrying out the role of parents. Even if our grandchildren don't live with us, we can influence them spiritually when they visit. If our adult children are following God, we can reinforce their godly values in our grandchildren's lives. But even if our children aren't obeying God, we can still make a strong, positive imprint on our grandchildren's lives.

*G*randpa taught me some of the same things my parents did, so his teaching reinforced my parents' values."
Joan, age 46

4. Read Deuteronomy 6:6–9 and underline the words that tell *when* to instruct our children (and in this case grandchildren) about God and prayer.

> *These commandments that I give you today are to be upon your hearts. Impress them on your children. Talk about them when you sit at home and when you walk along the road, when you lie down and when you get up. Tie them as symbols on your hands and bind them on your foreheads. Write them on the doorframes of your houses and on your gates.*

5. Now read the same passage from *The Message*, and underline the verbs that indicate *how* to instruct our grandchildren.

> *Write these commandments that I've given you today on your hearts. Get them inside of you and then get them inside your children. Talk about them wherever you are, sitting at home or walking in the street; talk about them from the time you get up in the morning to when you fall into bed at night. Tie them on your hands and foreheads as a reminder; inscribe them on the doorposts of your homes and on your city gates.*

6. List at least four times we are to instruct our grandchildren in the things of the Lord and prayer.

_____

_____

_____

_____

That's pretty much around the clock! These verses remind me of 1 Thessalonians 5:17: *"Pray without ceasing"* (KJV).

7. How can you intentionally teach your grandchildren to pray at these times? Can you add a few more?

When I sit at home _____

When we walk together _____

When I get up _____

When I go to bed _____

When I _____

When I _____

When I _____

One time while babysitting my two-year-old grandson Peter, I prayed aloud as we walked to the car. Peter looked up and appeared startled that I was praying as we walked. But he added his "amen" after mine.

Grandma Erna shared that she and her preschool-aged grandson are spontaneous about praying. When Max caught a small garden frog with Grandpa Bill's help, he came running to show his grandma the frog and said, "We've just got to stop right now and thank God for helping us catch this frog." After Max prayed, he ran off to catch more frogs. That evening he released his seven frogs into the apple orchard. His grandparents were thankful for the lessons in both biology and prayer.

To teach grandkids about prayer, seize the opportunities as they come. But also plan ahead and provide children's books, videotapes, and DVDs about prayer. With the parents' permission, we can give them to our grandkids as gifts or have them available in our homes. (See Appendix on page 211 for prayer resources.)

Also, most kids love to talk on the phone. Whether your grandchildren live nearby or far away, consider praying with them over the phone. Begin at a young age with simple prayers that show your love for God and them. For example, "Dear God, thank you for _____ (your grandchild's name). Give him/her a happy day and bless him/her."

This may feel unnatural at first, but try it. This way you'll establish a pattern of praying with your grandkids. As they get older, you can e-mail or text-message prayers. God answers both e-mail and knee-mail prayers! Then, when you see your grandchildren in person, praying together will seem natural.

As our grandchildren become older, they may prefer a more structured time to learn. One eighty-year-old grandpa met weekly with his teenage grandson for Bible study and prayer until the week before Grandpa died. Although his grandson didn't want to attend church youth-group meetings, he willingly learned about the life of Jesus from his grandpa. Of course, it didn't hurt that Grandma served his favorite home-cooked meals before the study.

Let's return to Jesus' teaching on the Lord's Prayer and further consider how prayer is taught. Entire books have been written on this Bible passage, but we'll limit our discussion to two questions.

> *We have many opportunities to weave prayer into our everyday, ordinary lives.*

> *Is prayer your steering wheel or your spare tire?" Corrie ten Boom*

8. Read Matthew 6:9–13 (NKJV), and beside each phrase, list how you could explain the meaning to your grandchild.

⁹Our Father in heaven, _____

Hallowed be Your name. _____

¹⁰Your kingdom come. _____

Your will be done _____

On earth as it is in heaven. _____

¹¹Give us this day our daily bread. _____

¹²And forgive us our debts, _____

As we forgive our debtors. _____

¹³And do not lead us into temptation, _____

But deliver us from the evil one. _____

For Yours is the kingdom and the power

and the glory forever. _____

Amen. _____

9. Based on the Lord's Prayer, what principles of prayer could you teach your grandchildren?

_____

_____

_____

_____

_____

I've listed what I'd like to teach my grandchildren based on Matthew 6:9–13.

Verse 9:   God wants to have a relationship with us. He is our heavenly Father and Friend.
God is holy, and we should praise Him in prayer.

Verse 10:   God is in control in Heaven and on Earth, and I want His will in my life.

Verse 11:   I can ask God for anything I need, and He will provide my needs.

Verse 12:   When I confess my sins, God forgives me.
God will help me forgive others.

Verse 13:   I can ask God to help me if I'm tempted or have a problem.
God has the power to help me.
God always deserves my praise and thanks.

We've only scratched the surface on prayer and what we can teach our grandchildren. But don't let that stop you from getting started. Your grandchild probably didn't score a goal the first time he or she kicked a soccer ball. Nor do you need to master all the skills of prayer to begin teaching your grandchildren. Resolve to model the reality of prayer in your daily life. Then as God directs and gives you opportunities, teach your grandchildren the simple essentials of prayer. You and your grandchildren can become mighty in prayer.

GRAND Thought: As we teach our grandchildren to pray, we are handing them a golden key that opens the door to a growing relationship with God for the rest of their lives.

Prayer: Dear heavenly Father, thank You for the gift of my grandchildren, and thank You for the gift of prayer. Both are such treasures. Open my eyes to see opportunities to model a spontaneous prayer life before my grandchildren. And give me creative wisdom to teach them ways to pray. From an early age, draw their tender hearts to love and obey You. Please guide me in my role as a grandparent. I'm available, Lord. Use me to teach my grandchildren to love talking to you in prayer.

Weekend Devotion

Good News!

I will pour out my Spirit on your offspring, and my blessing on your descendants. (Isaiah 44:3)

📖 Read: Isaiah 44:1–8

One morning I received good news. Our young grandson had become a Christian!

The night before, Peter had asked what his Awana memory verse meant: *"While we were still sinners, Christ died for us."* His mother explained Romans 5:8 and why Jesus died. Peter's questions continued, and then he prayed, "Jesus, keep me safe. I want to go to heaven. I want to follow Jesus." After a moment, he confidently added, "Jesus will come and pick me up and take me to heaven."

His mother explained that would happen someday, but

now he could follow Jesus by obeying the Bible. "If you want to follow Jesus, then you're a Christian," she said. "Are you a Christian?"

"Yes," Peter said.

She tucked him in, saying, "Good night, little Christian."

He smiled and replied, "Good night, big Christian."

Months earlier I had considered what could make the year special. My conclusion: Peter's salvation. God answered my prayer and poured out his blessing on our descendants (Isaiah 44:3). Now Peter could say, *"I belong to the Lord"* (v. 5).

When I told my husband, he shouted, "Hallelujah! Praise the Lord!" We thanked God and celebrated with sparkling cider. God, who formed Peter in the womb (v. 2), had poured out his Spirit on him. We have no greater joy than to know that our children walk in truth (3 John 4). Now, we pray that Peter will become a strong witness for God, proclaiming, *"There is no other Rock: I know not one"* (Isaiah 44:8).

Prayer: Lord Almighty, thank You for the good news of salvation. Pour out Your Spirit, and use me to help my grandchildren and others find you as Redeemer and Savior.

Prepare to Model a Godly Life

(Not just as I say, but as I do)

As we left to see a fairy tale play with our young grandsons Peter and Alex, I realized we would barely get there on time.

Just then Grandpa spotted a gas station with low prices and pulled in. Getting gas took longer than expected, so Grandpa became frustrated and pulled away from the pump before we were buckled in. My criticism of him started one of our "discussions." Though we kept our voices low, our grandsons sensed our tension. From the back seat, six-year-old Peter blurted out, "That's enough!"

Then Grandpa realized he'd forgotten his $5.00 change, but it was too late to return. Our cheap gas had become costly—in more ways than one.

Later, we realized our squabbling had set a bad example. We apologized to each other and prayed for help to model godly behavior for our grandchildren.

The next time we saw our grandsons, I asked, "Do you remember when Grandpa and I were fussing in the car?"

"Yes," Peter said without hesitation. "And I said, 'That's enough!'"

"We shouldn't have behaved that way," I said. "Will you forgive us?"

Peter nodded and grinned.

Whether we realize it or not, our behavior makes a huge impact on our grandchildren. They watch, learn, and copy us—whether good or bad. We're never off duty.

When I asked dozens of grandparents what character traits they wanted to model for their grandchildren, they mentioned the fruit of the Spirit. So that's our focus this week.

Day One

Growing the Real Fruit of the Spirit

"Let's cook," our grandkids say as they head to the play corner and pretend to make food. Before long, Grandpa and I "sample" the plastic foods heaped on our plates and compliment the kids on their cooking. But no matter what they serve, it's all fake. There's no real food and no real fruit. We'll look at what the Bible says about fruit—the fruit of the Spirit—and learn how to produce real rather than fake fruit.

Heartwork

Even if you've often read about the fruit of the Spirit, let the following verses take on new meaning as you consider how to model these character traits for your grandchildren: *"But the fruit of the Spirit is love, joy, peace, patience, kindness, goodness, faithfulness, gentleness and self-control. Against such things there is no law"* (Galatians 5:22, 23).

Wouldn't you love these virtues in your life and theirs?

Verse 22 begins, *"But the fruit of the Spirit is . . ."*

1. Is *fruit* singular or plural? (Note the verb.)

_____

Since the verse includes nine different aspects of fruit, some people think the word is *fruits*. But fruit is singular. These character traits all go together. I picture them as a cluster of grapes. If I say, "Help yourself to some fruit," you don't need to pick one or two grapes and end up with only love and joy. You can take all nine as a whole bunch!

2. Who produces the fruit? _____

_____

It is not up to us to produce this *produce*; we cannot create these genuine God-like characteristics even if we try. All we can produce is fake fruit, which doesn't nourish anyone.

3. In John 15:1, 4, 5 Jesus emphasized bearing fruit. Read the verses and underline the words related to bearing fruit.

> *I am the true vine, and my Father is the gardener. . . . No branch can bear fruit by itself; it must remain in the vine. Neither can you bear fruit unless you remain in me. I am the vine; you are the branches. If a man remains in me and I in him, he will bear much fruit; apart from me you can do nothing.*

4. Circle the word *remain(s)* in this passage. Jesus reveals the secret for bearing fruit. What is it?

_____

_____

Note the contrast between a harvest produced through Jesus and one grown apart from Him. *"Yes, I am the vine; you are the branches. Those who remain in me, and I in them, will produce much fruit. For apart from me you can do nothing"* (John 15:5 NLT).

Nothing? Really nothing? Yes—nothing. To produce genuine fruit, we must plant ourselves in Christ and remain connected to Him. In other words, displaying the fruit of the Spirit in our own strength is not only difficult, it's *impossible!*

We can wear phony smiles and pretend we have love, joy, and peace. But if anyone squeezes or bumps our fruit, we may be touchy and bruise easily. And our response to challenging circumstances may reveal sour, immature, or rotten fruit.

Throughout this week we'll learn more about modeling each characteristic of genuine fruit. Let's look at an overview of this nine-in-one fruit and see how God, our divine Gardener, and Jesus the Vine model each aspect.

5. Match the fruit with the verse that tells how God and Jesus show these attributes. Write the correct letter from the verse in front of the fruit.

God and Jesus Model the Fruit of the Spirit

_____ Love

_____ Joy

_____ Peace

_____Patience

_____ Kindness

_____ Goodness

_____Faithfulness

_____ Gentleness

_____ Self-control

A. "Peace I leave with you; my peace I give you. I do not give to you as the world gives." (John 14:27)

B. "I say these things while I am still in the world, so that they may have the full measure of my joy within them." (John 17:13)

C. This is love: not that we loved God, but that he loved us and sent his Son as an atoning sacrifice for our sins. (1 John 4:10)

D. "I will cause all my goodness to pass in front of you, and I will proclaim my name, the LORD, in your presence." (Exodus 33:19)

E. The LORD your God is God; he is the faithful God. (Deuteronomy 7:9)

F. The Lord is not slow in keeping his promise, as some understand slowness. He is patient with you, not wanting anyone to perish, but everyone to come to repentance. (2 Peter 3:9)

G. But when the kindness and love of God our Savior appeared, he saved us, not because of righteous things we had done, but because of his mercy. (Titus 3:4, 5)

H. "When they hurled their insults at him, he did not retaliate; when he suffered, he made no threats. Instead he entrusted himself to him who judges justly" (1 Peter 2:23)

I. Take my yoke upon you and learn from me, for I am gentle and humble in heart. (Matthew 11:29)

God's very nature exemplifies the fruit of the Spirit. And He wants to transfer these traits into our lives so we reflect His character and remain in close fellowship with Him.

6. Circle which of these nine aspects of the fruit of the Spirit are most evident in your life now. Then check one or more you'd like to cultivate and strengthen.

But remember, producing real fruit is not about behavior modification—it means abiding in the Vine and letting God help us grow in each area.

GRAND Thought: Our grandkids watch our behavior and learn how to live the Christian life from our example. If we stay connected to the Vine, we'll model how to produce much fruit.

Cut a vine from a plant and lay it on the counter. How long does it take to wither? Keep the wilted vine nearby all week as a reminder of what happens when we're not connected to the true Vine.

Prayer: Heavenly Father, I praise You for Your love and patience with me. Even though I don't always stay connected to You, when I repent, You forgive me and welcome me back into close fellowship. Please help me remain rooted and established in You, so I have the power to live in the fullness of Your love. I want to model the fruit of the Spirit for my grandchildren. I know I can only produce much fruit as I remain in You, so I choose to stay connected to the true Vine. Thank You for helping me grow and produce good fruit.

(Based on Ephesians 3:17–19)

Love and Joy

Day Two

Grandma Barbara shared: "When my daughter and her husband went out of town, I stayed at their home to care for my three young grandsons. Unfortunately, I don't sleep well in a strange bed. So after two nights of little sleep, I longed for a good rest. That night, after lying awake for hours, sleep finally came. Then a little voice woke me: 'Come look, Grandma,' my grandson beckoned. I followed him to the hallway window. 'Look, snow!'

"The streetlight shone on huge flakes, making them sparkle. Everything looked still and beautiful. We don't often get snow in our area, and now God had sent extra-large flakes.

> God has poured out his love into our hearts by the Holy Spirit, whom he has given us.
> (Romans 5:5)

Huddled together, we silently watched the snow until we shivered with cold. Once snuggled back in bed, I felt glad I hadn't been grumpy with my grandson. Even though it took hours to fall asleep, I'm thankful we shared our special time."

Heartwork

> But the fruit of the Spirit is **love, joy,** peace, patience, kindness, goodness, faithfulness, gentleness and self-control. Against such things there is no law. (Galatians 5:22, 23, emphasis added)

Love

Today we'll focus on the first two attributes in this fruit cluster: love and joy, both of which Barbara and her grandson experienced that snowy night. As we abide in Christ, God forms these traits in us, and they spill over into our grandchildren's lives.

Love is a basic human need. Our grandchildren need love and acceptance from us. Love is also the first aspect of the fruit of the Spirit, and the rest of the traits flow from it.

> Each day, a good prayer is, "Lord, may Your Spirit in me produce genuine fruit today. Fill me with your love and joy as I remain in You."

1. Read 1 Corinthians 13:4–8 aloud for a biblical description of love:

> Love is patient, love is kind. It does not envy, it does not boast, it is not proud. It is not rude, it is not self-seeking, it is not easily angered, it keeps no record of wrongs. Love does not delight in evil but rejoices with the truth. It always protects, always trusts, always hopes, always perseveres. Love never fails.

Because these verses include sixteen characteristics of love, I call these traits the "sweet sixteen." When they operate in our lives, we'll be sweeter than any box of candy.

2. Since God is love, these qualities describe God and His perfect love for us. In the left column, I omitted the word *love* and wrote *God* at the top. Read through the chart aloud saying, "God is patient, God is kind," etc.

"Sweet Sixteen" Characteristics of Love

God is	Your name	Scale
. . . is patient	_____ never gives up	1-2-3-4-5
. . . is kind	_____ cares more for others than self	1-2-3-4-5
. . . does not envy	_____ doesn't want what someone else has	1-2-3-4-5
. . . does not boast	_____ doesn't strut	1-2-3-4-5
. . . is not proud	_____ doesn't have a swelled head	1-2-3-4-5
. . . is not rude	_____ doesn't force himself/herself on others	1-2-3-4-5
. . . is not self-seeking	_____ isn't always "me first"	1-2-3-4-5
. . . is not easily angered	_____ doesn't "fly off the handle"	1-2-3-4-5
. . . keeps no record of wrongs	_____ doesn't keep score of the sins of others	1-2-3-4-5
. . . does not delight in evil	_____ doesn't revel when others grovel	1-2-3-4-5
. . . rejoices with the truth	_____ takes pleasure in the flowering of truth	1-2-3-4-5
. . . bears all things (NASB)	_____ puts up with anything	1-2-3-4-5
. . . always trusts	_____ trusts God always	1-2-3-4-5
. . . always hopes	_____ always looks for the best	1-2-3-4-5
. . . always perseveres	_____ never looks back	1-2-3-4-5
. . . never fails	_____ keeps going to the end	1-2-3-4-5

3. In the middle column, you'll find the description of love from *The Message*. Read the qualities of love again and place your name in the blank before each characteristic so it becomes "(Your name) never gives up," etc. Then, on a scale of 1 to 5, with 5 being the highest, circle a number to rate yourself in showing each characteristic of love.

4. Which aspects of love do you need to develop? How can you better love your grandchildren and model God's love? Focus on one or two areas this week.

_____

_____

_____

When our young son became a Christian, he beamed and said, "I love everybody!" Love is a product of the Holy Spirit in us. John 13:35 says, *"By this all men will know that you are my disciples, if you love one another."* Our son is grown now with children of his own, but he continues to love God and others.

When Christ lives in us and we obey His Word, He produces genuine fruit that remains.

Grandpa Bill offers this advice about loving our grandchildren: "Jesus had time for little children and showed them love. Grandparents need to make time for their grandchildren, too. If you show them genuine love, you'll be a tremendous influence for good in their lives. Teach them lessons you've learned from the Bible, and they'll have a better compass to make decisions."

Joy

God is also a God of joy.

When I pulled into my grandkids' driveway, I felt too tired to babysit. "Lord, please give me strength," I prayed. As I opened the car door, I heard music and saw the grandkids framed in the doorway, dressed in costumes. They were excited to see me and began dancing to a favorite song about having fun with Grandma. Since I often make them custard, I smiled when the lyrics included eating Grandma's delicious custard. Almost instantly, God replaced my weariness with joy, and we had a fun evening together.

Since joy is not based on circumstances, God's Spirit can energize us with joy even when we feel too tired to babysit. It's fun to be around bubbly, happy grandkids. But no matter what their personality or mood, I call them my "joy-bringers."

Because of God's Spirit in us, we can experience genuine joy even when we're not happy. Happiness is based on good things happening. But Christ-centered joy remains deep within even when we feel sad. Since I'm melancholy in temperament, I don't bounce around like Tigger, but I do sense God's joy in my heart.

"Happiness is based on chance; joy is based on choice. It's my choice to rejoice." (Message given by Pastor John Czech, June 2009, Northshore Baptist Church)

5. The following chart lists things that can steal our joy along with verses to gain victory in these areas. Check those you struggle with. Then list actions you can take to restore joy.

Take Joy!

	Joy Busters	Victory Verses	Actions to Restore Joy
	Anxiety	*Do not be anxious about anything, but in everything, by prayer and petition, with thanksgiving, present your requests to God.* (Philippians 4:6)	
	Fear and Dread	*He will have no fear of bad news; his heart is steadfast, trusting in the LORD.* (Psalm 112:7)	
	Negative or Critical Attitude	*"Do not judge, and you will not be judged. Do not condemn, and you will not be condemned. Forgive, and you will be forgiven."* (Luke 6:37)	
	What if . . . ? Worries	*Therefore do not worry about tomorrow, for tomorrow will worry about itself. Each day has enough trouble of its own.* (Matthew 6:34)	
	If Only . . . Regrets	*But one thing I do: Forgetting what is behind and straining toward what is ahead, I press on toward the goal to win the prize for which God has called me heavenward in Christ Jesus.* (Philippians 3:13, 14)	
	Resentment and Unforgiveness	*Bear with each other and forgive whatever grievances you may have against one another. Forgive as the Lord forgave you.* (Colossians 3:13)	
	Selfishness	*Each of you should look not only to your own interests, but also to the interests of others.* (Philippians 2:4)	

Despair	*Rejoice in the LORD, you who are righteous, and praise his holy name.* (Psalm 97:12)	
Hidden Sin	*Blessed is the man whose sin the LORD does not count against him and in whose spirit is no deceit. When I kept silent, my bones wasted away through my groaning all day long.* (Psalm 32:2, 3)	
Listening to Daily News Reports	*Whatever is true, whatever is noble, whatever is right, whatever is pure, whatever is lovely, whatever is admirable—if anything is excellent or praiseworthy—think about such things.* (Philippians 4:8)	
Disappointment with Grandkids	*Love . . . bears all things, believes all things, hopes all things, endures all things.* (1 Corinthians 13:4, 7 NASB)	

Here are specific actions other grandparents take to deal with joy busters.

Worry: I wrote out Philippians 4:6 and taped it to my computer. I also remind myself that God is in control, so I can relax.

Negative or critical attitude: I covenanted with God not to say anything critical and asked my friends to hold me accountable.

Dread: When I fear the future, I take my thoughts captive and choose to focus on today. I quote Psalm

112:7 and thank God He is with me, is trustworthy, and will provide fresh grace each day.

Fear: I keep a small metal cross near my desk to hold in my hand. When I have something challenging to do, I put the cross in my pocket to remind me Christ died for me and will give me strength.

Hidden sin: I ask God to search my heart. Then I confess what He reveals and thank Him I'm forgiven (1 John 1:9).

News reports: I stopped listening to the news on TV. I found alternative sources with more balanced reporting.

Disappointment with grandkids: I pray for them and their parents and trust God to handle disappointments. He sees the whole picture.

GRAND Thought: God delights to display His luscious fruit through us. If we stay connected to the Vine, God's love and joy will flow through us to our grandchildren.

Prayer: Heavenly Father, thank You for Your abiding love and joy. I want to model these qualities for my grandchildren. Please help me become more like You so my words and actions demonstrate love that is patient and kind. Help me to not be rude, conceited, or self-centered. Instead, may I rejoice in the truth and seek to protect, trust, hope, and persevere, so my love endures and never fails. And may Your genuine joy be visible to those around me.

(Based on 1 Corinthians 13:4–8)

> My first grandchild was born out of marriage, and my second grandchild was a step-grandchild. Both grandchildren have been a joy. I would advise grandparents to focus on the child, not their birth circumstances."
> Grandma Debbie

"What's peace?" I asked my husband. But before he could answer I said jokingly, "Is it when the grandkids go home?"

"No," he replied quickly. "It's too quiet when they're gone."

Do you sometimes feel tension between the joy of spending time with your grandkids and the peace and rest that come after they leave? I've heard grandparents say, "I love to see them come, but I also love to see them go."

Today we'll focus on two words in the list that begin with the same letter—peace and patience. They go together like two peas in a pod.

Heartwork

> *But the fruit of the Spirit is love, joy,* **peace**, **patience**, *kindness, goodness, faithfulness, gentleness and self-control.* (Galatians 5:22, 23, emphasis added)

Peace

What is real peace? Perhaps you've seen the saying, "Know God, know peace. No God, no peace." Peace begins with God and a relationship with Him through Jesus. To experience peace in our families, first we need to make eternal peace with God. Peace *with* God comes before we can experience the peace *of* God. If you have never made peace with God, you'll find steps to begin a relationship with Him in the Appendix on page 209.

God has many names. One is "Jehovah Shalom: The Lord is Peace." This name appears in the Old Testament when Gideon encounters God. *"But the LORD said to him, 'Peace! Do not be afraid. You are not going to die.' So Gideon built an altar to the LORD there and called it The LORD is Peace"* (Judges 6:23, 24).

When we trust God and believe He is in control, He gives us more than peace with Him. We also have peace within ourselves and peace in our relationships.

1. Read the following "peace promises" and match them with the descriptions. Write the letter in the blank in front of the verse.

Peace Promises

Verses	Qualities of God's Peace
_____ John 14:27 *Peace I leave with you; my peace I give you. I do not give to you as the world gives. Do not let your hearts be troubled and do not be afraid.*	**A.** Peace is a blessing from God. **E.** Peace comes from loving God's Word. Nothing can make us stumble when we focus on Him.
_____ Philippians 4:7 *And the peace of God, which transcends all understanding, will guard your hearts and your minds in Christ Jesus.*	**C.** Peace comes by trusting God. Focus on God, not self.
_____ Psalm 29:11 *The LORD gives strength to his people; the LORD blesses his people with peace.*	**E.** God gives peace that is beyond understanding; it guards our hearts and minds. It replaces worry.
_____ Isaiah 26:3 *You will keep in perfect peace him whose mind is steadfast, because he trusts in you.*	**P.** Jesus gives peace that is out of this world. We don't need to be troubled or afraid. Jesus hasn't abandoned us. Peace was His parting gift.
_____ Psalm 119:165 *Great peace have they who love your law, and nothing can make them stumble.*	

(Hint: The letters spell P-E-A-C-E.)

2. Select one peace promise. Write it on a note card and memorize it this week.

3. The following verses encourage us to live in peace with others. Underline the rewards for living in peace. Apply these verses to grandparenting and fill in the second column. The first one is filled in as an example.

Verses	Apply to Grandparenting
Blessed are the peacemakers, for they will be _called sons of God_. (Matthew 5:9)	God blesses me and calls me His child if I seek to make peace. My grandchildren will be blessed as I lead a life that shows peace with God and others.
Peacemakers who sow in peace raise a harvest of righteousness. (James 3:18)	
Live in peace. And the God of love and peace will be with you. (2 Corinthians 13:11)	
Let the peace of Christ rule in your hearts, since as members of one body you were called to peace. And be thankful. (Colossians 3:15)	
Make every effort to live in peace with all men and to be holy; without holiness no one will see the Lord. (Hebrews 12:14)	
Finally, all of you, live in harmony with one another; be sympathetic, love as brothers, be compassionate and humble. (1 Peter 3:8)	

Peace doesn't mean we won't have problems. Relationships involve conflict. In John 16:33, Jesus says, _"I have told you these things, so that in me you may have peace. In this world you will have trouble. But take heart! I have overcome the world."_

Is there an area where you need to trust God and receive His peace?

4. My husband and I both prefer peaceful surroundings, so we try to prevent or squelch squabbles when our grandkids visit. This isn't always possible, but the following ideas help us minimize fighting and quarreling.

Check ideas you want to try:

Ideas to Make Grandkids' Visits Peaceful

1. Prepare your heart before they come. Pray for them and the time you'll share.
2. Plan fun and constructive things to do together.
3. Create orderly, peaceful surroundings.
4. Play Christian music. It changes the atmosphere, and often the lyrics sink in.
5. Divide and conquer. When grandkids don't get along, separate them and do different activities with each of them.
6. Change the pace by showing a Christian videotape or DVD. Check them out at your church or public library or purchase some at Christian bookstores.
7. Memorize a peace promise together and explain its meaning.
8. Model peace in your actions and attitudes.
9. Realize that things won't always be peaceful. Work together with grandchildren to resolve problems in loving ways. Accept and forgive each other.

Add your own ideas:

_____

_____

_____

_____

> *We're either trusting or troubled. If we're troubled, we're not trusting. If we trust God and believe all things are under His control, we'll have peace. Trust equals peace."*
> *Pastor John Czech*

One of my favorite ideas for creating a peaceful home is to play Christian music.

When our three older grandkids came for a sleepover, the next morning I found Alex and Clara in the playroom doctoring the dolls and teddy bears. "Where's Peter?" I asked.

"He's resting," Clara said.

Resting? He had just eaten breakfast after a long night's sleep. I walked past the living room and saw Peter sitting in the rocker. With his head bowed, eyes closed, and hands folded, he listened to children's

> **From the lips of children . . . you have ordained praise.**
> **(Psalm 8:2)**

worship music. I wanted to get my camera and take a photo, but it seemed a holy moment, so I tiptoed away.

Later I felt God whisper, "If you prepare a worshipping atmosphere, they might worship."

Patience

Now that we're brimming with love, joy, and peace, let's focus on patience. Peace and patience belong together.

Both Old and New Testaments contain stories of parents and grandparents who waited to have children. Let's learn from the story of Hannah.

5. Read 1 Samuel 1:1–8 and watch the drama unfold. Then answer the questions below.

> *There was a certain man . . . whose name was Elkanah . . . He had two wives; one was called Hannah and the other Peninnah. Peninnah had children, but Hannah had none. Year after year this man went up from his town to worship and sacrifice to the LORD Almighty at Shiloh, . . . Whenever the day came for Elkanah to sacrifice, he would give portions of the meat to his wife Peninnah and to all her sons and daughters. But to Hannah he gave a double portion because he loved her, and the LORD had closed her womb. And because the LORD had closed her womb, her rival kept provoking her in order to irritate her. This went on year after year. Whenever Hannah went up to the house of the LORD, her rival provoked her till she wept and would not eat. Elkanah her husband would say to her, "Hannah, why are you weeping? Why don't you eat? Why are you downhearted? Don't I mean more to you than ten sons?"*

Hannah yearned to cradle a son, but God had closed her womb (v. 5). To make matters worse, the "other woman" was a fertile Myrtle and needled Hannah year after year because Hannah was barren.[4]

So we find Hannah in the tabernacle pouring out her heart's desire to God:

> *In bitterness of soul Hannah wept much and prayed to the LORD. And she made a vow, saying, "O LORD Almighty, if you will only look upon your servant's misery*

*and remember me, and not forget your servant but give
her a son, then I will give him to the L*ORD *for all the days
of his life."* (1 Samuel 1:10, 11)

Hannah made a tremendous vow to God, promising to give her son back to Him. How did God respond to her prayer?

> *So in the course of time Hannah conceived and gave
> birth to a son. She named him Samuel, saying, "Because
> I asked the L*ORD *for him."* (1 Samuel 1:20)

---

6. From this story, what can we learn about patience and God's timing?

Hannah had to develop patience in her circumstances, with God, with others, and probably with herself. What choice did she have? Babies take time, and first God had to open her womb.

You'll find the rest of the story in 1 Samuel, chapter 1. Hannah kept her vow. After she weaned Samuel, he lived in the temple with Eli. God used her much-prayed-for son to accomplish great things in the nation of Israel.

7. Is there a situation in your life in which you're waiting with hope for God to fulfill a desire of your heart? If so, jot down your thoughts.

We all enter a waiting room in life at some time, and we're told to "Please wait." I admit it—I'm *not* pleased to wait. Often God's timing doesn't match ours. But if we cooperate with God, He will mature this fruit in our lives.

8. The Bible uses words other than *patience* to indicate waiting a long time. In the verses below, underline the words *patient, patience, endurance,* and *perseverance.* Then apply these verses to grandparenting and fill in the third column. The first one is completed as an example.

Truths about Patience	Patience Verses	Apply to Grandparenting
Patience comes from God.	*Being strengthened with all power according to his glorious might so that you may have great <u>endurance</u> and <u>patience.</u>* (Colossians 1:11)	I can ask God for patience with my grandchildren.
We need patience for Christian living.	*Imitate those who through faith and patience inherit what has been promised.* (Hebrews 6:12)	
Our patience should be visible to others.	*Be patient, then, brothers, until the Lord's coming. See how the farmer waits for the land to yield its valuable crop and how patient he is for the autumn and spring rains.* (James 5:7)	
Patience is linked with love.	*Be completely humble and gentle; be patient, bearing with one another in love.* (Ephesians 4:2)	
Patience is part of suffering.	*Not only so, but we also rejoice in our sufferings, because we know that suffering produces perseverance; perseverance, character; and character, hope.* (Romans 5:3, 4)	

It takes patience to be a grandparent. Some grandparents are waiting for their first grandchild to be born, or even conceived. Others, with grandchildren who live continents away, are waiting for the next visit with their grandchildren. And if your grandchildren live nearby, you'll probably have opportunities to be patient with a fussy grandbaby, a toddler who spills milk, or a preschooler who dawdles on a walk.

Our grandchildren will learn about patience firsthand as they watch us handle life in patient or impatient ways. Throughout our lives, we'll continue to learn patience as we relate to God, others, ourselves, and our circumstances. *"But if we hope for what we do not see, with perseverance we wait eagerly for it"* (Romans 8:25 NASB).

GRAND Thought: It takes time for the seeds of peace and patience to blossom and develop into mature fruit in our lives. Let's be patient with ourselves. God is.

Prayer: Dear Lord, peace and patience are such appealing aspects of Your Spirit. But in my own strength, I struggle to display them. Challenges in life disturb my peace, and irritating situations test my patience. Fill me with Your Spirit so these qualities are evident in my life. Help me grow in You, so I reflect Your peace and patience to my grandchildren.

> *The* Never-Give-Up Family
> Patience
> Steadfastness
> Longsuffering
> Perseverance
> Tenacity
> Stamina
> Endurance
>
> *(Based on a message by Pastor Jan David Hettinga, January 30, 1994)*

Kindness and Goodness

Day Four

Grandma Dianna shared: "When my granddaughter Brittany was five, she loved to draw pictures for my refrigerator. But when she made new ones, I threw the old ones away. One day when she and her mom stopped by, Brittany found her pictures in the wastebasket.

"'Grandma, you're a liar!' she exploded in anger. 'You said you loved my pictures.'

"I felt brokenhearted for crushing her. 'I *do* love your pictures,' I said and hugged her. 'I'm sorry I didn't save the others when I put up new ones.' Overlooking her unkind words, I said gently, 'I'm disappointed with myself for hurting you. I'll work on my kindness.' This lesson made such an impression that I've saved nearly every paper since. Brittany no longer draws pictures for my refrigerator. But, at eighteen, she knows I love her and that she can trust me."

Heartwork

> *But the fruit of the Spirit is love, joy, peace, patience,* ***kindness, goodness****, faithfulness, gentleness and self-control.* (Galatians 5:22, 23, emphasis added)

Kindness

It's easy to say or do things that feel unkind to our grand-kids. To my regret, I've said and done things I didn't realize would hurt them. Thankfully, God forgives me, and so do they. Today we'll focus on kindness and goodness.

God's Word is filled with examples of kindness. Look for them as you read the Bible, and share them with your grand-children. We'll examine one together—the story of the Good Samaritan in Luke 10:30–37. It makes a great story to role-play with grandchildren. If you don't have enough people for each role, take turns playing the different characters.

Here's the background information:

Setting:	A 17-mile (two-day) trip on a treacherous road filled with robbers and thieves.
Priest:	Levite who served in the temple by offering sacrifices and prayers for God's people.
Levite:	Priest's assistant who took care of the temple. Only Levites could become priests, but not all Levites became priests.
Samaritan:	Lived in Samaria and was a person the Jews despised. The Jews considered Samaritans unclean.

1. Let's set the stage with the dialogue between a lawyer and Jesus in Luke 10:25–29, and then read through the story. I've written it in play format.

THE GOOD SAMARITAN

NARRATOR: On one occasion an expert in the law stood up to test Jesus.

LAWYER: Teacher, what must I do to inherit eternal life?

JESUS: What is written in the Law? How do you read it?

LAWYER: "Love the Lord your God with all your heart and with all your soul and with all your strength and with all your mind"; and, "Love your neighbor as yourself."

JESUS: You have answered correctly. Do this and you will live.

LAWYER: *(to justify himself)* And who is my neighbor?

JESUS: A man was going down from Jerusalem to Jericho, when he fell into the hands of robbers. They stripped him of his clothes, beat him, and went away, leaving him half dead.

A priest happened to be going down the same road, and when he saw the man, he passed by on the other side.

So too, a Levite, when he came to the place and saw him, passed by on the other side.

But a Samaritan, as he traveled, came where the man was; and when he saw him, he took pity on him. He went to him and bandaged his wounds, pouring on oil and wine. Then he put the man on his own donkey, took him to an inn and took care of him.

The next day he took out two silver coins and gave them to the innkeeper. "Look after him," he said, "and when I return, I will reimburse you for any extra expense you may have."

Which of these three do you think was a neighbor to the man who fell into the hands of robbers?

LAWYER: The one who had mercy on him.

JESUS: Go and do likewise.

If you role-play the story, you could act it out as one continuous story. Or divide it into scenes and let the narrator add background information.

Since the lawyer was well versed in the Law, he quoted parts of two verses in his reply to Jesus:

> *Love the LORD your God with all your heart and with all your soul and with all your strength.* (Deuteronomy 6:5)

> *Do not seek revenge or bear a grudge against one of your people, but love your neighbor as yourself. I am the LORD.* (Leviticus 19:18)

But God desires more of us than only *knowing* the law.

2. What was Jesus' four-word punch line at the end of the story?

_____

The Good Samaritan was willing to inconvenience himself, stoop down, and get bloody to help a stranger who was a Jew and probably hated him. Out of compassion he invested time, energy, and money to save the injured man's life. Meanwhile, the religious leaders, whom you would expect to help, had callously walked past on the other side of the road.

3. What would it look like for you to "go and do likewise" as you treat your grandchildren with kindness?

_____

_____

_____

4. Let's be honest. Even though we dearly love our grandkids, sometimes it's difficult to show kindness. Check situations when you would find it hard to be kind to your grandchildren.

When . . .

_____ I'm tired and crabby

_____ I'm ill or in pain

_____ I feel overworked

_____ I'm busy and they interrupt me

_____ I have to change my schedule to meet their needs

_____ They misbehave, fight, and argue

_____ They are unkind to me and don't deserve kindness

_____ They are disobedient

_____ Other_____

In my own strength, I wouldn't be kind in any of those situations. A *natural* response of the flesh is to *not* show kindness when it's inconvenient. But if we surrender to God and obey Him, He produces the *supernatural* fruit of kindness in our lives.

This leads to the next aspect of fruit: goodness. Kindness and goodness go together like twins. When we allow God's Spirit to work through us, kindness and goodness become evident.

Goodness

Perhaps you've heard someone say, "She's such a good person." Often this compliment is based on an individual's humanitarian actions. But that definition of goodness represents a worldly view. It doesn't reflect biblical truth. The truth is, apart from Christ, we have no goodness.

5. How does Isaiah 64:6 describe our deeds when done apart from a relationship with Christ? *"We are all infected and impure with sin. When we display our righteous deeds, they are nothing but filthy rags"* (NLT).

_____

Filthy rags stink! From God's viewpoint, actions done apart from Him also smell. Until we accept the free gift of Jesus and allow God's control in our lives, we have no goodness in ourselves. But there's *good* news!

6. According to 2 Corinthians 2:14, 15, how do our actions smell if we're in Christ?

> *But thanks be to God, who always leads us in trium-phal procession in Christ and through us spreads every-*

where the fragrance of the knowledge of him. For we are to God the aroma of Christ among those who are being saved and those who are perishing.

_____

_____

What a contrast! Aren't you glad your works don't need to smell like dirty rags? Because Christ loved us and became *"for us as a fragrant offering and sacrifice to God"* (Ephesians 5:2), we are a fragrant aroma to *"those who are being saved"* (2 Corinthians 2:15).

Of our five senses, the sense of smell leaves the strongest impression. When I smell Old Spice aftershave lotion, it reminds me of my father. When we show goodness to others, it should remind them of Jesus and the "fragrance of the knowledge of him" (v. 14).

Let's return to the story of the good Samaritan, which portrays both kindness and goodness. The lawyer first asks, *"Teacher, what must I do to inherit eternal life?"* Instead of answering his question, Jesus asks the lawyer questions that help him discover the answer for himself: *"What is written in the Law? How do you read it?"*

7. The lawyer quoted the law: *"'Love the Lord your God with all your heart and with all your soul and with all your strength and with all your mind'; and, 'Love your neighbor as yourself'"* (Luke 10:27).

Fill in the blanks below:

Love God with _____ and with _____
and with _____ and with _____
and love your neighbor _____.

Jesus agreed with the lawyer's answer and replied, *"You have answered correctly. Do this and you will live."*

The story could have ended there. But the lawyer asked another question that prompted Jesus to tell the parable of the good Samaritan. The concept behind the story is so familiar now that being a "good Samaritan" is associated with going out of your way to help others.

God instructs us to obey His Word. James 1:22 says, *"Do not merely listen to the word, and so deceive yourselves. Do what it says."*

Obeying God's Word requires action. Others will see God's goodness through our actions. The following chart contains verses that encourage us to *do* good works and to show God's goodness in us.

8. Read the following verses and circle the word *good* in each verse. Then answer the questions in the right-hand column.

"Good Works" Verses	Showing God's Goodness
Let us not become weary in doing good, for at the proper time we will reap a harvest if we do not give up. (Galatians 6:9)	We receive a reward for doing good. How and when do we get it? _____ _____
Therefore, as we have opportunity, let us do good to all people, especially to those who belong to the family of believers. (Galatians 6:10)	Every time we have a chance, we should do good. To whom? _____ _____
For we are God's workmanship, created in Christ Jesus to do good works, which God prepared in advance for us to do. (Ephesians 2:10)	God created us to do good works. When did he plan the good works He wants us to do? _____ _____
Command them to do good, to be rich in good deeds, and to be generous and willing to share. (1 Timothy 6:18)	We're commanded to do good; it's not an option. In what ways can we do good? _____ _____

9. Ask God, "What good works can I do for my grandchildren this week?" Even if distance separates you, you could call them, send a note or gift, e-mail them, or spend extra time praying for the fruit of the Spirit to grow in their lives. List what God prompts you to do.

_____

_____

_____

GRAND Thought: Kindness and goodness create a fragrant aroma in our lives that will draw our grandchildren and others to Jesus.

Prayer: Heavenly Father, I pray that Your kindness and goodness will flow through me to others. Help me to be rich in good works, especially to my grandchildren. Show me how to love them well so together we glorify You. (Based on 1 Timothy 6:18)

Day Five — Faithfulness, Gentleness, and Self-Control

We've studied the fruit of the Spirit and tried on various aspects of this nine-in-one fruit. We outfitted ourselves with love, joy, and peace—the one-syllable traits—and then put on two-syllable virtues—patience, kindness, and goodness. Today we'll conclude the week with the three-syllable aspects of the fruit of the Spirit—the **faithfulness** of God the Father, the **gentleness** of Jesus the Lamb of God, and the **self-control** the Holy Spirit provides.

Heartwork

> *But the fruit of the Spirit is love, joy, peace, patience, kindness, goodness, **faithfulness, gentleness** and **self-control**.* (Galatians 5:22, 23, emphasis added)

Faithfulness—God

From beginning to end, the Bible includes verses and stories about faithfulness. Most show God's faithfulness to us. Others deal with our faithfulness to God. I've gathered a small sample of verses below.

1. Read the verses and fill in the blanks about God's faithfulness and our response.

Faithfulness

God is _____.	*God, who has called you into fellowship with his Son Jesus Christ our Lord, is faithful. (1 Corinthians 1:9)* *He who promised is faithful. (Hebrews 10:23)*
God's faithfulness never _____. He always keeps His word.	*Your kingdom is an everlasting kingdom, and your dominion endures through all generations. The LORD is faithful to all his promises and loving toward all he has made. (Psalm 145:13)* *If we are faithless, he will remain faithful, for he cannot disown himself. (2 Timothy 2:13)*
God deserves _____ for His faithfulness.	*The living—they praise you, as I am doing today; fathers tell their children about your faithfulness. (Isaiah 38:19)* *With my mouth I will make your faithfulness known through all generations. (Psalm 89:1)*
God requires _____ from us.	*Now it is required that those who have been given a trust must prove faithful. (1 Corinthians 4:2)*
God _____ faithfulness.	*The LORD rewards every man for his righteousness and faithfulness. (1 Samuel 26:23)* *Be faithful, even to the point of death, and I will give you the crown of life. (Revelation 2:10)*
God's faithfulness strengthens and _____ us.	*He will cover you with his feathers, and under his wings you will find refuge; his faithfulness will be your shield and rampart. (Psalm 91:4)* *But the Lord is faithful, and he will strengthen and protect you from the evil one. (2 Thessalonians 3:3)*

I love the faithfulness of God. He has made thousands of promises and keeps them all. I can always count on Him. But can He count on me?

It can be difficult to keep our promises and finish assignments in the big areas of life, such as marriage, jobs, and grandparenting. Even small situations create a challenge to remain faithful, because faithfulness sometimes involves sacrifice. But it's worth the effort to set a positive example for our grandkids.

> *Faithfulness is evident in your life when you keep your vows, promises, and agreements (Ecclesiastes 5:4) and finish assignments you accept (1 Corinthians 4:2)." Pastor Jan David Hettinga*

Judy, now married thirty-three years, shared, "It took my husband and me ten years to work out our marriage problems. But I'm so glad we did. Now we're eager to welcome our first grandchild and grandparent him together."

As grandparents, we can model faithfulness and also teach it. Grandma Dianna said, "In Sunday school I challenged the kids to do a task they didn't like, and to faithfully continue until finished. My six-year-old granddaughter, Annie, chose to help her mom with daily kitchen duties for a week. Her mom loved the help, and Annie learned a lesson in faithfulness."

God is faithful and wants us to follow His example. Faithful people are reliable, trustworthy, and loyal. They keep promises and follow through with commitments. The good news is: When we remain in the Vine, His faithfulness flows through us.

Faithfulness is not about starting a race. It's about continuing and finishing well. A life of faithfulness is not like a short sprint. Instead, faithfulness is a long, steady-paced marathon—and it requires endurance. *"Let us throw off everything that hinders and the sin that so easily entangles, and let us run with perseverance the race marked out for us"* (Hebrews 12:1).

2. Choose a verse from the previous chart that will encourage you to model faithfulness to your grandchildren. Write it on a card, memorize it, and post it where you'll see it often.

Gentleness—Jesus

Picture a grandfather's strong hand gently holding his grandchild's small hand. The grandfather would never prove his strength by crushing the child's hand in a tight grip. Though he has strength, he controls it and shows tenderness as he holds his precious grandchild's hand. That's gentleness—strength under control.[5]

Jesus—the second member of the Godhead, who came as

the gentle Lamb of God—models gentleness. Both the Old and New Testaments speak of Him as gentle and how He cooperated with God's plan to redeem us, even sacrificing His own life. *"Look, the Lamb of God, who takes away the sin of the world!"* (John 1:29).

3. Read the following verses about Jesus and underline the words *gentle* and *gently*. Also underline words and actions of Jesus that show His gentleness.

The Gentleness of Jesus

Old Testament Prophecies	New Testament Verses
See, your king comes to you, righteous and having salvation, gentle and riding on a donkey, on a colt, the foal of a donkey. (Zechariah 9:9) *He was oppressed and afflicted, yet he did not open his mouth; he was led like a lamb to the slaughter, and as a sheep before her shearers is silent, so he did not open his mouth.* (Isaiah 53:7) *He tends his flock like a shepherd: He gathers the lambs in his arms and carries them close to his heart; he gently leads those that have young.* (Isaiah 40:11)	*'See, your king comes to you, gentle and riding on a donkey.'* (Matthew 21:5) *"Come to me, all you who are weary and burdened, and I will give you rest. Take my yoke upon you and learn from me, for I am gentle and humble in heart, and you will find rest for your souls."* (Matthew 11:28, 29) *"O Jerusalem, Jerusalem, you who kill the prophets and stone those sent to you, how often I have longed to gather your children together, as a hen gathers her chicks under her wings, but you were not willing!"* (Luke 13:34)

Jesus set an example of gentleness in words and actions, and He wants us to "follow the Leader" and model gentleness to our grandchildren.

4. Read the following verses, underlining the words *gentle* and *gentleness*. What can we learn from them and apply to grandparenting? The first one is filled in as an example.

Let your <u>gentleness</u> be evident to all. The Lord is near. (Philippians 4:5)	My gentleness should be obvious to my grandchildren and others.
Be completely humble and gentle; be patient, bearing with one another in love. (Ephesians 4:2)	
Clothe yourselves with compassion, kindness, humility, gentleness and patience. (Colossians 3:12)	
As apostles of Christ we could have been a burden to you, but we were gentle among you, like a mother caring for her little children. (1 Thessalonians 2:6, 7)	
But you, man of God, flee from all this, and pursue righteousness, godliness, faith, love, endurance and gentleness. (1 Timothy 6:11)	

My mother, Lena, set an example of gentleness and passed it down to the following generations. Lena gave birth to her third son in a Russian hospital while her husband was in prison for preaching the gospel. They escaped to America in 1931, and raised a family during the Depression. During her lifetime, she buried three children and experienced miscarriages. But hard times made her strong, not hard. How blessed we were to have a mother and grandmother who displayed gentleness!

If a grandchild found an injured bird, Grandma Lena got an eye-dropper and taught the child how to feed the baby bird. Grandma couldn't let anyone suffer. There was always enough love and gentleness where Grandma was." Ann

Lena's granddaughter Joan said, "Grandma was warm, soft, and cuddly. I always wanted to sit next to her and put my head on her shoulder. I felt loved and secure when I was with her. She made me cuddly things—soft stuffed animals and quilts. At age 46, I still snuggle in the childhood quilt she made me. It reminds me of my sweet, gentle grandma's love." It probably won't surprise you that Joan named her firstborn Lena.

Even if we don't have earthly role models of gentleness, we have Jesus to follow. And we ourselves can model gentleness for our children and grandchildren.

5. Specifically, what does gentleness look like in our relationships with our grandchildren?

_____

_____

_____

Prayer: Father, I long to reflect the gentleness of Jesus. I want these words to describe me: mild, tender, gracious, kind, even-tempered, balanced, tranquil, reasonable, forbearing, fair, considerate, willing to pardon, and someone who rules my spirit well. Please help me follow in the gentle footsteps of Jesus. Let the words of my mouth and the mediations of my heart be pleasing to You—because they are graced with gentleness. (Based on Psalm 19:14)

Self-Control—The Holy Spirit

We've come to the final aspect of the fruit of the Spirit—self-control.

From an early age, grandchildren say, "Me do it." They want control. But if we have *true* self-control, we're not in control—the Holy Spirit is.

The apostle Peter's life demonstrates how a rough fisherman became a powerful, self-controlled preacher. He also wrote two books of the Bible. God's Spirit within him created a genuine makeover! Enjoy these "before and after" clips from Peter's life.

> Since we live by the Spirit, let us keep in step with the Spirit. (Galatians 5:25)

THE "BEFORE" PICTURE

Scene 1: The Garden of Gethsemane

The disciples finished the Last Supper; Judas left to betray Jesus. Then Jesus and His disciples walked to the Garden of Gethsemane, and Jesus pleaded with God to remove the cup of death.

6. Picture yourself in the garden with Jesus and his disciples. The soldiers have come to arrest Jesus. Peter—our man of action—takes action!

> *Then Simon Peter, who had a sword, drew it and struck the high priest's servant, cutting off his right ear. Jesus commanded Peter, "Put your sword away! Shall I not drink the cup the Father has given me?"* (John 18:10, 11)

From this scene, how would you describe Peter's personality and actions?

_____

_____

Have you ever responded emotionally and in haste? Perhaps we can all identify with Peter's impetuous, vindictive spirit.

Scene 2: Peter denies Jesus three times

In Matthew's account, Jesus predicted what Peter would do. Put yourself in Peter's shoes and try to understand his thoughts and feelings.

> *Then Jesus told them, "This very night you will all fall away on account of me,"* . . . *Peter replied, "Even if all fall away on account of you, I never will." "I tell you the truth," Jesus answered, "this very night, before the rooster crows, you will disown me three times." But Peter declared, "Even if I have to die with you, I will never disown you."* (Matthew 26:31, 33–35)

Although Peter had good intentions, we know Jesus foretold Peter's actions correctly.

7. What can we learn about Peter's character from these verses?

_____

_____

Peter felt ashamed he had denied his wonderful friend. After Jesus died, Peter decided to return to his fishing career. But look what happened.

THE "AFTER" PICTURE

After Jesus' resurrection and the coming of the Holy Spirit, Peter became a different man. You might say he had an extreme makeover. Jesus forgave Peter for denying Him and gently restored him (John 21:15–17), and God's Spirit controlled Peter's actions. Let's look at two scenes after Peter's transformation.

Scene 3: Peter heals many

Instead of acting on impulse as he did in cutting off someone's ear, Peter shows quiet strength as he cares about others and heals people through the Spirit's power.

8. Underline why people brought the sick into the streets.

> *The apostles performed many miraculous signs and wonders among the people. . . . More and more men and women believed in the Lord and were added to their number. As a result, people brought the sick into the streets and laid them on beds and mats so that at least Peter's shadow might fall on some of them as he passed by.* (Acts 5:12, 14, 15)

In Acts 3:1–10, we read the exciting story of Peter healing the crippled beggar. His words to the beggar were: *"Silver or gold I do not have, but what I have I give you. In the name of Jesus Christ of Nazareth, walk"* (v. 6). And he did!

Scene 4: Peter preaches the gospel with power

Although Peter cowered and denied Jesus before Christ's crucifixion and resurrection, he later preached with boldness to the crowd who had killed Jesus. When he preached his first sermon (Acts 2:14–41), three thousand people came to know Jesus. What a revival!

God used Peter, now self-controlled, to become a powerful leader of the church. Acts 4:13 says, *"When they saw the courage of Peter and John and realized that they were unschooled, ordinary men, they were astonished and they took note that these men had been with Jesus."*

9. How could God use our weak traits or unique character-

istics when we surrender them to Him? In what specific ways can we demonstrate self-control to our grandchildren?

_____

_____

_____

We started this week with the aspect of love and now finish with self-control. Perhaps these two qualities are the bookends that hold all the other character traits together.[6]

GRAND Thought: The fruit we yield will be determined by how much we *yield* to the Holy Spirit.

Prayer: Heavenly Father, how we treasure the work of the Holy Spirit in us! We acknowledge that in our own strength, we cannot bear real fruit. But we can display this appealing fruit as we stay connected to the Vine. Please continue to transform us into Your image. Then our grandchildren will be blessed by the love, joy, peace, patience, kindness, goodness, faithfulness, gentleness, and self-control that overflow to them and are evident to all. We commit to follow You with wholehearted devotion and to model Jesus and the fruit of the Spirit to our grandchildren. Strengthen our faith, guide us to walk uprightly, and help us bear much fruit for Your glory.

> _I will not run my life, because when you add I to run, it becomes ruin." Grandma Tea_

Weekend Devotion

A Rock-Solid Foundation

Everyone then who hears these words of mine and acts on them will be like a wise man who built his house on the rock. (Matthew 7:24 ESV)

📖 Read: Matthew 7:24–29

"Another song," a sweet little voice begged from the back seat of the car. While driving our two-year-old granddaughter Clara home, my husband and I sang one Christian chorus after another. She enjoyed the words and the motions, and sometimes chimed in. As we sang, "The wise man built his house upon the rock," we paused to let her fill in words like *rock, sand,* and *crash.*

Singing Christian choruses with Clara made our travel time joyful and allowed us to plant seeds of spiritual truth in her life. But I also need to apply the lessons from the wise man and become a wise woman. According to Matthew 7, what does that mean?

Anyone knows that building a house on a rock foundation is preferable to building on sand. And everyone wants a home that withstands winds, storms, and rain. But these verses are not about building a physical home. They are about building a life on Jesus, the solid Rock. And when we do, God considers us wise; and we set a good example for our grandchildren.

But how can we know we're building wisely? According to verse 24, wise builders not only hear God's words, they also act on them. Their foundation is firm. But those who don't apply God's Word are like foolish carpenters, building on sand.

Today, I need to dig deeper and evaluate my life's foundation. Does it pass God's building code for a solid base? When the floods of adversity beat on me, I want my grandchildren to see through my life that "the house on the Rock stood firm."

Prayer: O Lord, You are my Rock, my firm Foundation. I want to build my life on You alone. Help me model a godly life for my grandchildren, so they also want to build their lives only on You.

Prepare to Invest in Their Lives

(Love is spelled T-I-M-E)

The eighteen-year-old triplets stood before guests to honor their grandparents, Al and Barbara, at their fiftieth anniversary. In a faltering voice, John spoke first. "You have always been there for me, in bad times and good times. Papa, I remember how you played baseball with me, even when your arm hurt. And you helped me with homework."

Courtney spoke next. "Grammie, you were like a second mother to me. You led me to God. Thank you very much. You are beautiful inside and out. I want to be just like you." She wiped tears and continued. "Papa, you guided me and believed in me. I remember our fishing trips. You're the best. I love you with all my heart."

Then Matthew added, "I remember our trips—sometimes a month long, traveling to Disneyland and several states. Our car broke down, but we had fun. And Papa, when we stayed overnight, you woke us by playing your guitar and singing."

Then the three hugged and kissed their grandparents, and everyone's eyes glistened with tears.

Since the triplets grew up in a single-parent home with a working mom, their grandparents helped raise them. Their mother dropped them off at 4:30 a.m. on the way to work. After the kids slept a few more hours, Al and Barbara fed them and took them to school. Obviously, the grandparents' investment of time and love made a strong impression on the triplets and shaped their lives for good.

According to a *Family Circus* cartoon, "Love is spelled T-I-M-E." This week we'll study ways to invest time and love into our grandchildren's lives.

What we invest (our time, love, and effort) determines our return.

Welcome to Grandma's House! *Day One*

I love the word *welcome*. It's a friendly, inviting word. So, welcome to another lesson. Today we'll focus on creating a home where our children and grandchildren feel welcome.

When I became a grandmother, my friend Hanne gave me a sign that hangs outside our front door. It says:

Grandma's Babysitting Service

Little people always welcome

Service includes
meals   lessons   entertainment
and lots of hugs

**Tender, loving care for your
most precious possessions**

Visitors smile when they read it. And on the front porch next to it sits a garage-sale wooden high chair with a big rag doll. It didn't cost much to create a child-friendly welcome.

Heartwork

The Bible is filled with examples of welcoming others— and that includes grandkids! But only five passages (NIV) use the word *hospitality*, which is a translation of the Greek word *philoxenia*. *Philos* means "loving," and *xenos* means "a stranger." So *hospitality* means "love of strangers" (*Expository Dictionary of New Testament Words* by W. E. Vine, 2:235 [4 vols]).

1. Read the five passages that mention the word *hospitality*. Then answer the questions below.

> *Share with God's people who are in need. Practice hospitality.* (Romans 12:13)

> *No widow may be put on the list of widows unless she is over sixty, has been faithful to her husband, and is well known for her good deeds, such as bringing up children, showing hospitality, washing the feet of the saints, helping those in trouble and devoting herself to all kinds of good deeds.* (1 Timothy 5:9, 10)

> *Now the overseer must be above reproach, the husband of but one wife, temperate, self-controlled, respectable, hospitable, able to teach, not given to drunkenness, not violent but gentle, not quarrelsome, not a lover of money.* (1 Timothy 3:2, 3)

> *Offer hospitality to one another without grumbling.* (1 Peter 4:9)

> *Since an overseer is entrusted with God's work . . . he must be hospitable, one who loves what is good, who is self-controlled, upright, holy and disciplined.* (Titus 1:7, 8)

Which passage says hospitality is a test of Christian character?

_____

In which two verses is hospitality commanded?

_____

Which two passages list hospitality as a requirement for church leadership?

_____

Some requirements for church leaders seem obvious. But I was surprised their "to do" list included hospitality. However, according to the verses in Romans and 1 Peter, hospitality is *not* an option—it's a command for everyone.

2. People give various reasons for not showing hospitality. Check ones you've heard or have felt.

_____ I don't have time.
_____ My home is too small.
_____ I feel embarrassed by my shabby furnishings.
_____ My home is too messy.
_____ I'm not a good cook.
_____ I'm not a people person.
_____ Other_____

I admit, I'm guilty of some of these excuses. My main obstacle is clutter. Often I don't notice the mess until the doorbell rings. Then I glance around and think, *Oh, no, I can't let them in!*

But even if my home isn't magazine perfect, I still enjoy company and have learned quick tricks to prepare for guests. Sometimes I grab a laundry basket and fill it with clutter and stash it in a closet. Other times I post a sign on the door of a messy room that says: "Danger. Keep out." You don't need a perfectly organized home to invite family and friends. Simply create a tidy corner and welcome guests into the prepared places.

If you would like to show hospitality more often, begin with your family. Perhaps that means inviting them for a meal, overnight, or even to live with you for a season.

"Our first grandchild was born outside of marriage. Mom and daughter lived with us for four years. When our granddaughter was three and my husband was out of town, she crawled into bed with me and fell asleep. When we awoke the next morning, all snuggled together, she said, 'Gramma, you and me got a good thing going.' It was true. And sixteen years later, we indeed have a good thing going!" Grandma Shirley

"When I'm with the grandchildren, I'm not too busy to spend time with them. I let them take turns staying overnight so they get one-on-one time with me." Grandma Dot

It takes time and preparation to open our hearts and homes. But when we do, we're following Jesus' example.

In John 14:2, 3, Jesus said, *"I am going there to prepare a place for you. And if I go and prepare a place for you, I will come back and take you to be with me that you also may be where I am."*

3. What does this verse say Jesus is doing for us right now?

_____

How can we follow His example as we relate to our grand-children?

_____

_____

_____

If your grandchildren don't live nearby, perhaps you know children who would love a surrogate grandparent. And wouldn't it comfort you if someone near your distant grand-children would grandparent them in your absence? Ask God, "Is there a child You want me to grandparent?" Here's the testimony of one mom with surrogate grandparents:

"Before my first baby was born, I felt sad that her grandparents lived far away. Longing for nearby grandparents, I wrote to a beloved couple from church without grandchildren, asking them to be my G.I.F.T. (Grandparents in Future Training). They were a won-derful gift with child care, love, and prayers. They also felt "gifted" by caring for baby Christine. When they moved away, God provided another G.I.F.T. An elderly widow babysat my daughter monthly as I prepared for another baby. She became the girls' extra grandma and was a wonderful resource and role model for me." Ann

4. According to the following verse, as you enrich a child's life, whom else do you welcome?

Whoever welcomes this little child in my name wel-comes me; and whoever welcomes me welcomes the one who sent me. (Luke 9:48)

_____

Now, let's get practical and discuss babysitting. In this study, we'll call it _grand-sitting_, because it's a lot _more_ than what we think of as babysitting. If your young grandchildren live nearby, you'll probably have opportunities to grand-sit.

5. Grandparents view grand-sitting from one end of the spectrum to the other. Compare the pros and cons, and check ones that express your feelings.

Pros

_____ I welcome it

_____ It's a choice

_____ It's a privilege

_____ It's a joy

_____ It's a blessing

_____ It's an eternal investment

_____ There's nothing I'd rather do

_____ It's a chance to love my kids and grandkids

_____ Other _____

Cons

_____ I dread it

_____ It's a duty

_____ It's an interruption

_____ It's a chore

_____ It's a burden

_____ It's a waste of my time

_____ I have better things to do

_____ They're taking advantage of me

Here are some grand-sitting comments from other grandparents:

"We spent Wednesdays with one grandson from infancy until school age. Oh, the adventures we had! We picked Tyler up in the morning and returned him at suppertime. His family said he swaggered and acted like a big shot when he came home. That's because we treated him like a little king. All the grandchildren have been little kings and queens." Great-Grandma Margaret

"Always be available to care for your grandchildren. It's fun and gives their parents time for a date. When our children had been married ten years, each couple took a long vacation, and we cared for their children. The grandchildren loved time with us, and their parents enjoyed a relaxing time." Grandpa Bill

"Set boundaries that suit you. Some grandparents feel they shouldn't be expected to babysit at a moment's notice, and others jump at any chance. Be yourself. Enjoy the time with your grandchildren. They're not a chore, but a gift—precious to God." Grandma Bonnie

Even though many grandparents are still working, they enjoy spending time with their grandchildren when they can. However, no grandparents want to be taken advantage of.

They want to feel appreciated. To avoid grand-sitting friction, consider these guidelines:

Grand-Sitting Guidelines

1. Respect each other. (Matthew 7:12)
2. Don't grand-sit if you feel resentful about it. (2 Corinthians 9:7)
3. Communicate your feelings to your children. Tell them you don't want to be taken for granted. (Ephesians 4:15)
4. Through prayer, determine your priorities. Then decide whether your actions reflect your priorities. (James 1:5)
5. Remember, grandchildren grow up fast. They won't beg for sleepovers when they're teenagers. Seize the moment! (Ecclesiastes 3:1)

We established this rule with our children: You can always ask. We can always say no. This gives us all freedom. We enjoy time with our grandchildren, but we don't change previous plans unless it's an emergency. Since our children have other grandparents nearby who grand-sit, we aren't called on too often. When we're needed, our children ask in advance. Mutual respect goes a long way.

6. What grand-sitting boundaries would you like to establish? Read these verses to help you decide. Record your insights after the verses.

> *'It is more blessed to give than to receive.'* (Acts 20:35)

> *Let us not become weary in doing good, for at the proper time we will reap a harvest if we do not give up. Therefore, as we have opportunity, let us do good to all people, especially to those who belong to the family of believers.* (Galatians 6:9, 10)

> *Do not withhold good from those who deserve it, when it is in your power to act.* (Proverbs 3:27)

> *God loves a cheerful giver.* (2 Corinthians 9:7)

> *"Grand-sitting pays in memories, not money. But the memories are far more precious than money."* Grandma Tea

I believe God wants me to develop this attitude toward grand-sitting:

_____

_____

_____

Considering my circumstances, I think these grand-sitting boundaries are wise:

_____

_____

_____

_____

_____

7. God told Abraham he was blessed to be a blessing (Genesis 12:1–3; 22:16–18). How has God blessed you? How can you provide a home that is welcoming and bless your grandchildren? (If you don't have grandchildren nearby, how can you "gift" someone else's grandchildren?)

_____

_____

_____

GRAND Thought: Don't wait for the ideal time to invest in your grandchildren's lives. It may never come. Welcome them into your life and home now, in the midst of all that's going on. Your grandchildren will be blessed, you'll be blessed, and God will bless you.

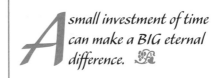

A small investment of time can make a BIG eternal difference.

Prayer: Heavenly Father, bless us as we invest in the lives of our grandchildren. Make our time with them truly wonderful—a real investment for eternity. Mold us into the grandparents You want us to be. I pray we won't resent the time spent with our grandchildren or see them as an interruption from more important work. Instead, help us realize that investing time and love into their lives *is* the real work You have prepared for us at this season. Father, You love and welcome children. May we follow Your example. (Based on Ephesians 2:10)

Join Their FAN Club

Grandma Barbara's story:

"Ready! Set! Go!" shouted the young man helping with the cross-country meet. My husband and I had come to watch our older grandsons run, but to our surprise, our three-year-old grandson, Ethan, was right behind them. Could he really run a half-mile?

We caught glimpses of Ethan's yellow shirt as he ran past the trees lining the track. When the spectators realized Ethan was really running the race, they began to cheer for him.

Soon most of the runners sprinted across the finish line. Then we saw Ethan's head appear over the ridge. Sweaty blond curls stuck to his forehead. People clapped as he crossed the finish line.

Later Ethan told his grandpa, "Everyone told me, 'Congratulations.' I think I won!"

Ethan felt like a winner because he had fans.

Every grandchild needs fans. Let's join their FAN clubs and become their:

> When five-year-old Clara and I had a snack together, she complimented me: "I don't always get along with my brother, but I get along with you." Grandma Tea 🌺

Friends
Affirmers
Nurturers

Heartwork

Friend: I'm here for you!

God created all of us to need friends and gave us His Son to be our Friend. So it's clear—our grandkids need friends. Let's learn from Solomon's wisdom and see how we can befriend our grandkids and "be there" for them.

1. What can you learn about the qualities of a *true* friend from the following verses? List your insights in the right column.

Friend Verses	A true friend is someone who:
A friend loves at all times, and a brother is born for adversity. (Proverbs 17:17)	
Perfume and incense bring joy to the heart, and the pleasantness of one's friend springs from his earnest counsel. (Proverbs 27:9)	
Do not forsake your friend and the friend of your father. (Proverbs 27:10)	
If one falls down, his friend can help him up. But pity the man who falls and has no one to help him up! (Ecclesiastes 4:10)	

Now let's learn from Jesus, the ultimate example of a perfect friend.

2. According to John 15:13–15, Jesus calls us His friends. Underline what Jesus did for us.

> *Greater love has no one than this, that he lay down his life for his friends. You are my friends if you do what I command. I no longer call you servants, because a servant does not know his master's business. Instead, I have called you friends, for everything that I learned from my Father I have made known to you.*

> *A grandparent with a good ear for listening becomes a real friend for young ones. The grandchildren believe Grandpa and Grandma know what they're talking about and have been through it all."*
> *Grandma Diana*

Some grandchildren may be easier to love than others. And it may be easier to love them more at different stages of their lives (and ours). If we have a hard time loving a grandchild and don't emotionally *feel* love for him or her, we can ask God to love this child through us. And though it may take time for our emotions to catch up so we *feel* like loving our grandchild, we can choose to start with loving actions. Our actions are like an engine that drives the train. Our feelings, like a caboose, tag along behind—later.

Do you have a grandchild who is hard to love? If so, daily ask God to love that child through you. Then watch Him work in your heart and through your actions. Through Him you can become your grandchild's dear friend.

In 2 Corinthians 12:19, Paul calls the Corinthians "dear friends" and says he wants to strengthen them. *"Everything we do, dear friends, is for your strengthening."*

3. Paul also calls the Philippians his "dear friends." What else does he call them? How does he feel toward them?

> *Therefore, my brothers, you whom I love and long for, my joy and crown, that is how you should stand firm in the Lord, dear friends!* (Philippians 4:1)

_____

_____

_____

Since our grandchildren are called our "crowns" in Proverbs 17:6, it's precious to see the link between a crown and a friend in Philippians 4:1. And yes, they are also our joy!

4. What kind of friend would you like to be to your grandchild? Write a prayer, asking God to help you become that kind of friend. Also, consider writing your grandchild a "Dear Friend" letter.

_____

_____

_____

_____

Affirmer: You can do it!

The "A" in F**A**N stands for Affirmer. Everyone needs affirmation.

In the Bible, Barnabas is a wonderful example of an affirmer.

5. Underline the meaning of Barnabas' name found in Acts 4:36, 37.

> *Joseph, a Levite from Cyprus, whom the apostles called Barnabas (which means Son of Encouragement), sold a field he owned and brought the money and put it at the apostles' feet.*

In the verse above, we read how Barnabas encouraged the Jerusalem church by providing the money the church needed. But he also encouraged Saul as a new convert.[7]

6. According to Acts 9:26–28, what did Barnabas do for Saul?

> *When he [Saul] came to Jerusalem, he tried to join the disciples, but they were all afraid of him, not believing that he really was a disciple. But Barnabas took him and brought him to the apostles. He told them how Saul on his journey had seen the Lord and that the Lord had spoken to him, and how in Damascus he had preached fearlessly in the name of Jesus. So Saul stayed with them and moved about freely in Jerusalem, speaking boldly in the name of the Lord.*

_____

_____

_____

In Acts 15:36–41, we learn that Barnabas also believed in his cousin, John Mark (Colossians 4:10) and gave him a second chance after his failed missionary work. Paul didn't want to take John Mark along because of his previous lack of commitment. But Barnabas had confidence in John Mark and took him along on his journey.

Wouldn't you love an encouraging friend like Barnabas—someone who provided monetary support by selling his possessions, vouched for you when others were suspicious of your reputation, and believed in you and gave you a second chance? Our grandchildren would, too.

How can we become this type of affirming friend to our grandchildren?

In school, young children often bring their favorite belongings for "show and tell." As grandparents, we can find ways to "show and tell" our grandkids how special they are.

7. The chart below lists ideas from A to Z to affirm your grandkids. Read the affirming action and Bible verse for each letter. Then list specific ways to apply these ideas to your grandkids. Select five or more letters to fill in now. Then come

back during the following weeks to complete the chart. For example, for *Accept,* you could:

- Write a prayer asking God to help you accept each grandchild.
- Write affirming words to show that you accept them, such as, "I like you just the way God made you."
- List a specific time to affirm your grandchild by a specific action. For example, "When I take _____ to lunch, I'll tell her how special she is."

The ABCs of Affirming Your Grandchildren

	Affirming Actions	Bible Verses	Apply to Your Grandkids
A	Accept each child as a unique individual created in God's image.	*I praise you because I am fearfully and wonderfully made.* (Psalm 139:14)	
B	Believe in them and their potential.	*I can do everything through him who gives me strength.* (Philippians 4:13)	
C	Compliment them for their efforts, accomplishments, and character development.	*I always thank God for you because of his grace given you.* (1 Corinthians 1:4)	
D	Delight to spend time with them.	*I long to see you, so that I may be filled with joy.* (2 Timothy 1:4)	
E	Encourage them through your words and actions.	*Encourage one another and build each other up.* (1 Thessalonians 5:11)	
F	Forgive their mistakes and ask forgiveness for yours. Show unconditional love.	*Forgive whatever grievances you may have against one another.* (Colossians 3:13)	
G	Give them room to grow and change.	*There is a time for everything, and a season for every activity.* (Ecclesiastes 3:1)	

H	**H**ug them and show affection in various ways.	*We were gentle among you, like a mother caring for her little children. We loved you so much.* (1 Thessalonians 2:7–8)	
I	**I**nvest time in them and identify with their interests.	*I have no one else like him, who takes a genuine interest in your welfare.* (Philippians 2:20)	
J	**J**oin their FAN club. Attend their special events and cheer them on.	*I remind you to fan into flame the gift of God, which is in you.* (2 Timothy 1:6)	
K	**K**eep your eyes on the big picture rather than on petty annoyances.	*Set your minds on things above, not on earthly things.* (Colossians 3:2)	
L	**L**isten to them with your heart. Show that you value them and are interested in what they say and do.	*Everyone should be quick to listen, slow to speak and slow to become angry.* (James 1:19)	
M	**M**entor them. Look for ways to teach and encourage them.	*Let us . . . spur one another on toward love and good deeds.* (Hebrews 10:24)	
N	**N**otice their strengths and the things they do right. Avoid criticism and faultfinding.	*Whatever is lovely . . . admirable . . . praiseworthy . . . think about such things.* (Philippians 4:8)	
O	**O**ffer support; come alongside them during hard times.	*Carry each other's burdens, and in this way you will fulfill the law of Christ.* (Galatians 6:2)	
P	**P**ray for them daily— without fail.	*Night and day I constantly remember you in my prayers.* (2 Timothy 1:3)	
Q	**Q**uiet their hearts with God's Word when they're troubled.	*"Do not let your hearts be troubled. Trust in God."* (John 14:1)	

R	**R**emind them of God's love and good plans for their lives.	*For I know the plans I have for you . . . to give you hope and a future.* (Jeremiah 29:11)	
S	**S**peak kind words with a gentle tone of voice. Let your words be honey for their hearts.	*Let your conversation be always full of grace.* (Colossians 4:6) *Pursue . . . gentleness.* (1 Timothy 6:11)	
T	**T**reasure them for who they are. Thank God for them.	*For everything God created is good, and nothing is to be rejected.* (1 Timothy 4:4)	
U	**U**nderstand their individual needs and recognize their differences from others.	*Do nothing out of favoritism.* (1 Timothy 5:21)	
V	**V**isualize achievement for them. Value them and their interests.	*My God will meet all your needs according to his glorious riches in Christ Jesus.* (Philippians 4:19)	
W	**W**elcome them like you would welcome Jesus Himself.	*"Whatever you did for one of the least of these brothers of mine, you did for me."* (Matthew 25:40)	
X	e**X**plain God's Word and answer their spiritual questions.	*"Were not our hearts burning within us while he talked with us on the road and opened the Scriptures to us?"* (Luke 24:32)	
Y	**Y**ield your personal desires in order to focus on their interests.	*Each of you should look not only to your own interests, but also to the interests of others.* (Philippians 2:4)	
Z	**Z**ero in on ways to make them feel loved and to help them reach their potential.	*We are God's workmanship, created in Christ Jesus to do good works . . . prepared in advance.* (Ephesians 2:10)	

8. Now choose five of the affirming actions that you just filled out (e.g., Encourage, Hug, Listen, Treasure, and Pray) and list them below. Also list ideas how you will apply them to your grandchildren. If possible, implement one this week.

1. _____

2. _____

3. _____

4. _____

5. _____

Now we'll hit the pause button and save the last letter of FAN for tomorrow.

GRAND Thought: It's a privilege to join our grandchildren's FAN clubs. God smiles when we invest in their lives and become their friends.

Prayer: Heavenly Father, thank You that Jesus gave up His life so I could have a relationship with You and be Your friend. Thank You also for the example of Barnabas, who encouraged others. Show me ways to encourage my grandchildren, born or yet to be born. Work in my heart and through my life, so my words and actions build my grandkids up and draw them to You. Thank You for the gift of grandchildren and the privilege of investing in their lives.

Nurture Friendship

Day Three

We've come to the "N" in FA**N**. Besides needing us as friends and affirmers, our grandchildren also need us to nurture them and help them grow. We'll focus on nurturing them through our affection and by helping them develop interests and skills. We'll save spiritual nurturing for the next lesson.

Heartwork

Nurturer: Let me help you grow.

In the book of 1 Thessalonians, the apostle Paul reveals his shepherd's heart. After Paul and Silas planted a fledgling church in Thessalonica, opposition to the gospel arose, and they fled for their lives. Paul and Silas tried to return many times to nurture the new converts but Satan prevented them (1 Thessalonians 2:18). Since Paul couldn't be with them, he wrote this letter instead.[8]

1. Read the verses in the left-hand column and underline words that express Paul's affection and concern for the Thessalonians. The first one has been completed as an example. We'll come back to the right-hand column later.

Scripture Verses	Grandparenting Words and Actions
We were _gentle_ among you, like a _mother caring_ for her little children. We _loved you so much_ that we were _delighted to share_ with you not only the gospel of God but our lives as well, because you had become so _dear to us._ (1 Thessalonians 2:7, 8)	Show gentleness, like a mother. Care for my grandkids as little children. Love them. Delight in sharing the gospel with them. Share my life with them. Tell them they are dear to me. Write to them if I can't be with them.
For you know that we dealt with each of you as a father deals with his own children, encouraging, comforting and urging you to live lives worthy of God, who calls you into his kingdom and glory. (1 Thessalonians 2:11, 12)	
But, brothers, when we were torn away from you for a short time (in person, not in thought), out of our intense longing we made every effort to see you. (1 Thessalonians 2:17)	
How can we thank God enough for you in return for all the joy we have in the presence of our God because of you? Night and day we pray most earnestly that we may see you again and supply what is lacking in your faith. (1 Thessalonians 3:9, 10)	

2. Re-read the verses, but this time read them from the perspective of a grandparent nurturing a grandchild. What can we learn and apply from Paul's words and actions? The first one is completed as an example.

Does it surprise you that Paul, the man who persecuted Christians before his conversion, now writes such tender, affectionate words? Perhaps we would expect this zealous, learned former Pharisee to write a harsh, intellectual letter. But Paul combines the gentleness of a nursing mother with the comfort and affirmation of a doting father. I love his warm, tenderhearted approach. Paul, transformed by God and inspired by the Holy Spirit, shows us that we all—both men and women—can express compassionate caring and become nurturers. Isn't that how we long to love our grandkids?[9]

> *What I like about my grandparents is they are generous, kind, and loving. I like to be around them." Julia, age 10*

Paul demonstrates similar love to the churches in Rome, Corinth, and other cities, as well as in letters to specific individuals, such as Philemon, Titus, and Timothy. If adults and church groups need nurturing, our grandchildren certainly do, too.

3. What areas do you believe are key in nurturing your grandchildren? Read the following promises, and check ones you want to work on. Add others important to you.

Promises to My Grandchildren

A. I will accept you as you are and love you unconditionally.

"Accept one another, then, just as Christ accepted you, in order to bring praise to God" (Romans 15:7).

B. I will treat you with respect and never deliberately embarrass or belittle you.

"Show proper respect to everyone" (1 Peter 2:17).

C. I will speak to you in kind, considerate ways. No ridicule, name-calling, or criticism.

"A gentle answer turns away wrath, but a harsh word stirs up anger" (Proverbs 15:1).

D. I will forgive your mistakes and ask forgiveness for mine.
   "Forgive us our debts, as we also have forgiven our debtors" (Matthew 6:12).

E. I will spend quality time with you and take time to listen.
   "Out of our intense longing we made every effort to see you" (1 Thessalonians 2:17).

F. I will give you freedom to be yourself and develop your potential.
   "We have different gifts, according to the grace given us" (Romans 12:6).

G. My home will always be a safe haven for physical and emotional rest and security.
   "He who fears the LORD has a secure fortress, and for his children it will be a refuge" (Proverbs 14:26).

H. _____

_____

I. _____

_____

J. _____

_____

Now let's focus on another way to nurture our grandchildren.

Helping Grandkids Develop Skills and Talents

4. Read Exodus 35:31–35, and underline the different craftsmen and skills God used to build the tabernacle.

And he has filled him with the Spirit of God, with skill, ability and knowledge in all kinds of crafts—to make artistic designs for work in gold, silver and bronze, to cut and set stones, to work in wood and to engage in all kinds of artistic craftsmanship. And he has given both him and Oholiab son of Ahisamach, of the tribe of Dan, the ability to teach others. He has filled them with skill to do all kinds of work as craftsmen, designers, embroider-

ers in blue, purple and scarlet yarn and fine linen, and weavers—all of them master craftsmen and designers.

Just as God gave various gifts during the time of Moses, he also gifts us today with different skills. Since I'm a home economist, I like to cook and sew with my grandkids. My six-year-old granddaughter enjoys "helping" me sew pillows or blankets for her dolls and bears. One of my grandsons especially likes to bake and calls himself a "cookie artist."

What skills or interests do you have? Perhaps you enjoy gardening, music, or rock collecting. Do your grandchildren have similar interests? Look for their strengths and skills and nurture them. Proverbs 22:6 says, *"Train a child in the way he should go, and when he is old he will not turn from it."* This means to train them according to their bent—how God created them. Each grandchild is a surprise package, and as each one develops, it's exciting to unwrap more of the package and see the beautiful gifts inside.

5. List your interests, skills, and hobbies in the left-hand column. In the right-hand column, list ones your grandchildren might have.

> *What I like about Grandpa and Grandma is that they are always willing to listen to me. They are models in every way."* Andrew, age 11

Your interests, skills, and hobbies	Your grandchild's interests, skills, and hobbies

Which of your skills and hobbies could you teach your grandchildren?

6. Ask God to show you how to help your grandchildren develop their talents. Record your ideas here.

_____

_____

_____

_____

_____

One of the things I love most about Grandpa and Grandma is they always support us at band concerts and sports events." Jeff, age 12

These three roles—**F** (Friend), **A** (Affirmer), **N** (Nurturer)—blend together to make well-rounded grandparents. If we only develop one of them, it's like hitting a single in baseball. But when we accomplish all three, it's a homerun! You know you've hit a homerun when:

- You show up at your granddaughter's baseball game and she waves from across the field and yells, "Hi, Grandpa!"
- Your grandchild perks up when he hears your voice as you enter his hospital room.
- Your young grandchild squeals with delight when you serve his favorite food.
- Your grandchildren feel proud of their musical accomplishments because you helped pay for their instruments and lessons.

Here's a final true FAN club story from my life:

Crowds lined the streets, and noise and excitement filled the hot summer air. A young man had returned home as the winning contestant on a television show. Although my husband and I didn't watch that program, our kids and grandkids had followed the singer and were attending his homecoming. On the spur of the moment, we decided to meet our family there.

We found our clan in the crowd and chatted as we waited for this hometown hero. Fans chanted the winner's name and anticipated his arrival. Finally, a car with the local celebrity drove down the main street, and everyone waved signs and cheered.

After he passed by, I turned to our grandkids and said, "Everyone came to see (I can't even remember his name), but *we* came to see *you*."

My oldest grandson said, "But Grandma! I can't sing like that."

"It doesn't matter," I said. "You don't need to sing. We love you just as you are, and we like to spend time with you."

I'm not sure he understood. But no matter what, Grandpa and Grandma are co-presidents of his FAN club, and we'll cheer him on through life.

> *My grandchildren know I love them and like to see them. I always have time to give them attention." Grandpa Bill*

7. If you want to join your grandchild's **FAN** club, please complete this certificate. Or copy the FAN words in the middle and post them on your refrigerator.

FAN Club Certificate

This is to certify that _____
is a member in good standing of the FAN club for the grandchild(ren) named below:

_____
and is entitled to all the privileges of membership.
They include investing in a grandchild's life and becoming a first-rate

Friend: I'm here for you!
Affirmer: You can do it!
Nurturer: Let me help you grow!

Granted this _____ day of _____, in the year of

our Lord 20 _____.

Sealed with: *Being confident of this, that he who began a good work in you will carry it on to completion until the day of Christ Jesus.* (Philippians 1:6)

GRAND Thought: If you are in your grandchildren's FAN clubs they will know it—because your actions will show it! You will display their pictures on your refrigerator, and if you live near them, you'll be on the sidelines cheering them on. As you do, you'll imprint them with memories for life. From you, they will learn what a real FAN club member does. And someday, when *they* become grandparents, they'll join their grandkids' FAN club—because you joined theirs.

Prayer: Thank You, dear Lord, for the gift of grandchildren. They add such meaning and richness to my life. Teach me to affirm and nurture them and to develop a precious, lifelong friendship with them—not for selfish reasons such as what *I* get from it, but to help them become all You planned for them to be. Give me a deep affection for them and a strong desire to nurture them in their God-given talents and skills. Thank You that I can partner with You and invest in their lives. I'm available to love and nurture them. Please use me for Your glory and for Your kingdom.

Day Four

Spiritual Wisdom

When Grandpa Gord's grandsons were nine and ten, their father asked him to mentor them. So Gord began taking one of them to breakfast every other week.

Over pancakes and eggs, they discussed school, prayer requests, and Proverbs. After five years in Proverbs, they studied other passages in the Bible. Now his older grandson has graduated from high school and has moved to another city to work in missions.

Grandpa Gord also informally tells his grandchildren what God teaches him. And at his church, he started a "Grandpas to Go" program to encourage older men to nurture boys who don't have grandpas. "It doesn't take much preparation," he said, "just availability."

Heartwork

Availability. Time. One of the most powerful ways to invest time in our grandchildren's lives is by teaching them spiritual truths. If we have faithfully walked with God for years, we have much to share. But even if we're new in the faith, we still have wisdom to offer. Plus, the Holy Spirit within teaches us. *"But the Counselor, the Holy Spirit . . . will teach you all things and will remind you of everything I have said to you"* (John 14:26).

1. Read Deuteronomy 4:9 aloud, phrase by phrase. What does each phrase mean to you, and how can you apply each one as you teach your grandkids?

Only be careful, and watch yourselves closely . . .

_____

_____

_____

Do not forget the things your eyes have seen or let them slip from your heart . . .

_____

_____

_____

As long as you live.

_____

_____

_____

Teach them to your children and to their children after them.

_____

_____

_____

2. Choose a phrase from Deuteronomy 4:9 you want to focus on this week, and write it here.

_____

_____

_____

> Only be careful, and watch yourselves closely so that you do not forget the things your eyes have seen or let them slip from your heart as long as you live. Teach them to your children and to their children after them.
> (Deuteronomy 4:9)

For me, the first phrase, *"Be careful, and watch yourselves closely,"* is the most convicting. These words warn me that I must start by keeping *my* spiritual life in order. Otherwise, I won't have much to pass on.

When our grandsons came for a sleepover, they pretended to play war. I had recently studied 2 Chronicles 20 and said, "I read about an exciting battle in the Bible where three armies attacked Israel." I had their attention, so I told the story of how God defeated the Israelite's enemies and they didn't need to fight. "And it even took them three days to gather up the plunder," I added (and explained *plunder*).

"I know why it took three days," eight-year-old Alex said. "There were three armies, so one day for each army." I smiled, knowing he had listened.

As I remain in God's Word, I'll have fresh stories to share during teachable moments.

3. Shortly before his death, Moses reminded the children of Israel of the Ten Commandments and passed on important teaching. What is his main message in Deuteronomy 6:1, 2?

> *These are the commands, decrees and laws the LORD your God directed me to teach you to observe in the land that you are crossing the Jordan to possess, so that you, your children and their children after them may fear the LORD your God as long as you live by keeping all his decrees and commands that I give you, and so that you may enjoy long life.*

_____

_____

_____

4. How many generations does Moses address?

_____

_____

5. What is the reward for obedience?

_____

_____

6. As grandparents, how can we practically live out Deuteronomy 6:1, 2?

_____

_____

_____

_____

Before I studied these passages, I didn't realize God's

Word commands us to teach our grandchildren. Did you? But now that we know, it's important to make a commitment to teach them—and to be *consistent* and *intentional* about sharing spiritual truths.

For some, time and/or distance make it difficult to meet face-to-face with grandchildren. And some parents may not want their children taught the Bible. But whether our grandchildren live near or far, or in Christian homes or not, we *can be certain* God wants them to know Him. Second Peter 3:9 says, *"He is patient with you, not wanting anyone to perish, but everyone to come to repentance."*

I imagine some may say, "But you don't know my situation." No, I don't, but God does. In Mark 10:27, Jesus said, *"All things are possible with God."* Let's not limit God or give up on sharing the Bible with our grandchildren. God wants to help us obey Him in this area.

Let's get practical. *What* should we teach? The entire Bible is full of God's truth. With young children, start with Bible storybooks and verses about God's love. With older children, perhaps you'll teach from Proverbs as Grandpa Gord did. Depending on your grandchild's age, you could study another book of the Bible together, such as John or Philippians.

It's not only very important *what* we teach our grandchildren, it's also important *how* we teach them. Jesus is the master Teacher. As you read the Bible, especially the Gospels, look for His methods. Jesus told stories and parables and also used illustrations of everyday things the people understood, such as vineyards, bread, and coins. As we spend time with our grandchildren in everyday situations, we can apply His teaching methods and others I've put into a chart below.

7. Read the tips, verses, and specific examples of how to apply them. Add your ideas in the third column.

> When our first child was two, an elderly man I respected said, 'Be sure you enjoy her each day because she won't be young long.' I took his advice, and to any grandparents I say, 'Teach and enjoy your grandchildren now, because time flies, and your grandchildren won't be young long.'" Grandpa Bill

> Max (age 4) remembered stories of the Israelites going to a land flowing with milk and honey, so he tried an experiment, putting together milk and honey. He thought it tasted delicious." Grandma Erna

Tips for Teaching

Tips	Verses	Apply
Seize teachable moments to share God's truth.	*These commandments that I give you today are to be upon your hearts. Impress them on your children. Talk about them when you sit at home and when you walk along the road, when you lie down and when you get up.* (Deuteronomy 6:6, 7)	Read Bible stories at bedtime. Discuss a topic when it comes up even if you weren't planning to.
Make learning fun.	*Our mouths were filled with laughter, our tongues with songs of joy.* (Psalm 126:2)	Use object lessons, drama, music, crafts, games, and cooking. Plan family nights and include spiritual lessons.
Tell stories that teach lessons.	For example, the Prodigal Son (Luke 15:11–32), or the Good Samaritan (Luke 10:25–37).	Share stories from the Bible, from your personal life, and from other family members.
Repeat biblical principles to help them remember.	*My son, do not forget my teaching, but keep my commands in your heart.* (Proverbs 3:1)	If you want your grandkids to know that God loves them, keep telling them, and *show* His love to them.
Help them experience the lesson to remember it.	*He [Jesus] called a little child and had him stand among them.* (Matthew 18:2)	If you're teaching patience, make yeast bread and let them wait for it to rise and bake.
Use age-appropriate content and length.	*When I was a child, I talked like a child, I thought like a child, I reasoned like a child.* (1 Corinthians 13:11)	Use short stories and simple words for young children.
Set a good example by your life.	*Let your light shine before men, that they may see your good deeds and praise your Father in heaven.* (Matthew 5:16)	Show them that the Christian life is practical, and God's Word is your light.

We've focused on teaching our grandchildren. But we certainly don't have all the answers. Our grandchildren also have plenty to teach *us*. When Jesus taught about humility, He said, *"Whoever humbles himself like this child is the greatest in the kingdom of heaven"* (Matthew 18:4).

In Matthew 11:25, Jesus says, *"I praise you, Father, Lord of heaven and earth, because you have hidden these things from the wise and learned, and revealed them to little children."*

8. What could our grandchildren teach us?

_____

_____

_____

_____

_____

9. Since this lesson emphasized teaching, I'll end with a short quiz. I'm sure you'll get 100 percent right. Check the true statements.

_____ 1. It's not my job to teach my grandchildren spiritual truths. That's the job of their parents and the church.

_____ 2. The more time I spend with my grandkids, the more opportunities I'll have to teach them on an informal basis.

_____ 3. Since kids like to play church, it would be a good idea to set up a pulpit in my living room, sit my grandkids in a row, and preach to them.

_____ 4. Children aren't ready to learn until they are school age, so I can wait until my grandchildren are in kindergarten before sharing Bible wisdom.

_____ 5. God's Word specifically commands me to teach my grandchildren.

(Answers: 2 and 5 are true.)

GRAND Thought: It's a privilege to teach our grandchildren Bible truths. And when we do, we're obeying God's command.

Prayer: Dear Lord,
Let my teaching fall like rain
and my words descend like dew,
like showers on new grass,
like abundant rain on tender plants.
I will proclaim the name of the LORD.
Oh, praise the greatness of our God!

Yes, Lord, please use my teaching and my example to help my grandchildren ("tender plants") become like well-watered gardens, and like springs that never fail. And may their roots go down deep into the soil of Your love. Give them teachable hearts, so they will delight in Your law and become like trees planted by streams of water, which yield fruit in season. I pray their leaves will not wither, and whatever they do will prosper. Lord, these "tender plants" are dear to me and You. I accept Your mandate to teach them. Let Your Word flow through me as I help them grow and flourish.

(Based on Deuteronomy 32:2, 3; Isaiah 58:11; Ephesians 3:17 [NLT]; Psalm 1:2, 3)

Day Five — Financial Giving

My grandkids love treasure hunts. Whether they search for plastic eggs filled with surprises or follow clues that lead to a hidden treasure chest with gifts, they are eager to search—because it's fun, and the reward is worth it. Sometimes I give them small garden spades to literally dig in the dirt to find treasure (money wrapped in plastic bags).

Today we're going on a treasure hunt. I hope you're eager to dig into God's Word and search for principles of giving we can apply to grandparenting.

Heartwork

In 2 Corinthians, Paul devotes two chapters to financial giving and encourages generosity. He commends the Macedonian churches for their sacrificial giving and challenges the Corinthians to complete their earlier commitment to help needy Christians in Jerusalem.

1. As you read 2 Corinthians 8:1–12, circle the word *grace* and underline words related to giving. Enjoy this word search for hidden treasure.

1 And now, brothers, we want you to know about the grace that God has given the Macedonian churches.

2 Out of the most severe trial, their overflowing joy and their extreme poverty welled up in rich generosity.

3 For I testify that they gave as much as they were able, and even beyond their ability. Entirely on their own,

4 they urgently pleaded with us for the privilege of sharing in this service to the saints.

5 And they did not do as we expected, but they gave themselves first to the Lord and then to us in keeping with God's will.

6 So we urged Titus, since he had earlier made a beginning, to bring also to completion this act of grace on your part.

7 But just as you excel in everything—in faith, in speech, in knowledge, in complete earnestness and in your love for us—see that you also excel in this grace of giving.

8 I am not commanding you, but I want to test the sincerity of your love by comparing it with the earnestness of others.

9 For you know the grace of our Lord Jesus Christ, that though he was rich, yet for your sakes he became poor, so that you through his poverty might become rich.

10 And here is my advice about what is best for you in this matter: Last year you were the first not only to give but also to have the desire to do so.

11 Now finish the work, so that your eager willingness to do it may be matched by your completion of it, according to your means.

12 For if the willingness is there, the gift is acceptable according to what one has, not according to what he does not have.

2. Now examine this passage for clues about giving. In these questions, *they* refers to the Macedonian churches.

Verse 2: Even though poor and suffering trials, they gave

_____

Verse 3: Without being forced, they gave

_____

Verse 4: They pleaded to give and considered it

_____

Verse 5: They didn't do the expected. First they gave

_____

These verses don't deal with specific amounts. Instead they reflect heart attitudes. Because the Macedonians gave themselves to God first (v. 5), they recognized His ownership of all they had and realized they were God's stewards.

If we believe everything we have belongs to us, that's ownership. If we view our possessions as loaned to us by God, to use for His purposes, that's stewardship.

3. Look at verses 6 and 7 to discover the relationship between giving and grace. How does God's grace impact our attitude toward financial giving?

_____

_____

In verse 7, what six things does God's grace produce?

1. _____
2. _____
3. _____
4. _____
5. _____
6. _____

Since we are born with a selfish nature, it's no wonder we need God's grace to produce sacrificial giving. In our own strength, we are unable to invest in the lives of others. If we do give, we may be motivated by law or duty rather than a response to God's grace.

4. Let's contrast the difference between giving produced by God's grace and giving motivated by law. Read the following statements and mark each with an L for law or G for grace.

_____ I give so others will accept me.
_____ I give because God has accepted me.
_____ I give because it's a privilege to give.

_____ I give out of duty.

_____ I give as little as I can.

_____ I give as much as I can.

_____ I give because I enjoy giving.

_____ I give because I have to.

_____ My giving shows stinginess.

_____ My giving reflects gratitude to God.

> For where your treasure is, there will your heart be also. (Matthew 6:21 KJV)

5. Where on this grid would you put your heart attitude toward giving?

Law (I have to)—1—2—3—4—5—6—7—8—9—10—Grace (I get to)

6. What can we learn from Jesus' example of giving in verse 9?

Jesus was _____, but for us He became _____.

We were _____, but because of Jesus we are _____.

7. In verses 10–12, Paul gives straightforward advice. List the verse numbers where he tells us:

Finish the giving you started. _____

Give with eager willingness. _____

Give according to your means. _____

If you're willing, that's what counts. _____

Give according to what you have, not what you don't have. _____

As we get older, perhaps we're more willing to give. Instead of gathering, we're downsizing. Our focus may become less temporal and more eternal.

8. You've been digging hard, and by now you've found several clues for scriptural giving. The following chart lists principles of giving along with examples of how to apply them. Check the ones you want to apply. In the blank spaces at the end of the chart, add additional principles and treasures you find.

> Your present treasure influences where your heart will be in the future. What is your treasure right now? Where is it leading you?

Generous Giving
(Based on 2 Corinthians 8)

Verses	Principles of Giving	Treasures for Grandparenting
1, 2, 6, 7	Because of God's grace at work in our lives, even in poverty, we can give generously.	Giving goes beyond money. I can give generously of my time, love, wisdom, and creativity.
2, 4	Be eager to give without being asked.	If I sense a need, I'll ask my kids or grandkids, "How can I help?"
5	If we first give *ourselves* to God to do His will, other giving will follow.	Pray, "Lord, here I am, ready to do Your will. Show me how to bless my grandchildren."
9	To benefit others, follow Christ's example of sacrificial giving.	Whether there is a financial, emotional, or spiritual need, I can open my heart and wallet to help my grandchildren.
11, 12	No matter the size of our gift, it is acceptable to God if we willingly give what we have.	If my grandchildren have a need I can meet, I will give with a willing heart.
2, 3, 5, 12	Generosity is admirable, but we need to balance generosity and good stewardship.	I'll resist overspending and give in moderation, according to their needs.

Our spiritual gifts (Romans 12:6–8) may influence our desire to invest financially in our grandchildren's lives. Those with the gift of giving may feel greater motivation to give than those with other gifts.

Our love languages can also influence our desire to give. Grandparents whose primary love language is gifts may want to express their love by giving to their grandchildren. In my family of origin, my mother always wanted to give money and gifts to the grandchildren. But my father thought the money should go toward missionaries. My mother, who normally let her husband make decisions, wouldn't back down in this area. My parents did give generously to missions, but Mother also made certain her twelve grandkids received gifts for birthdays and Christmas. If she were still alive, I'm certain she would make sure her twenty-three great-grandchildren also received gifts.

9. These specific examples show how various grandparents invested financially in their grandchildren from birth to adulthood. As the grandparents gave, they also expressed love. Check those you would also like to do.

> *When my five-year-old grandson visited, he found an inexpensive doll I had purchased. He had a blast playing with it and asked, "Gramma, can you really afford all these toys and food?" I said, "Why do I get the toys?" He said, "Because you love me." Grandma Erna*

- Helped prepare their grandchild's nursery by painting, wallpapering, and sewing curtains and crib bumpers.
- Hosted a baby shower to welcome the grandbaby.
- Purchased major items for the baby, such as a crib and a stroller.
- Watched for bargains at garage sales and bought a high chair, port-a-crib, and toys to make their home grandchild-friendly.
- Hired their grandchildren to work for them to earn money.
- Bought the grandchild a musical instrument the parents couldn't afford.
- Helped pay for their grandchildren's Christian education.
- Purchased back-to-school clothes for grandchildren.
- Took the grandkids on a surprise trip to Disneyland.
- Planned ahead and saved money to help pay for their grandchildren's college education.
- Loaned the grandchild's parents money to purchase an adequate home for their growing family.

The amount we financially invest in our grandchildren's lives is an individual matter, and it may vary according to their needs and our assets. If we wonder what is appropriate to

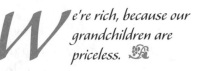

> *We're rich, because our grandchildren are priceless.*

> *When we invest financially, we commit money to earn a future financial return. As we sow generously into the lives of our grandchildren, we look forward to future benefits in their lives.*

give, a trusted friend may be able to offer wise counsel.

As we give ourselves and all we have to God and pray for wisdom, He will guide us in what to give. One grandmother advises, "If you have prayed about what to do and both grandparents agree, do it. Then watch what God will do with your giving."

GRAND Thought: *"Each man should give what he has decided in his heart to give, not reluctantly or under compulsion, for God loves a cheerful giver"* (2 Corinthians 9:7). The best gift you can give is your time and yourself.

Prayer: Heavenly Father, help me give with joy, so I please You and bless my grandchildren.

Weekend Devotion

Hold Me!

How priceless is your unfailing love! Both high and low among men find refuge in the shadow of your wings. (Psalm 36:7)

Read: Psalm 36:5–10

When my husband and I were grand-sitting our two grandchildren, my husband played pretend games with two-and-a-half-year-old Clara. Meanwhile, I tried to keep two-month-old Owen happy by holding him and rocking him. When their mom returned a few hours later, I handed Owen to her. Clara immediately looked up at me and asked, "Do you want to hold me?"

I didn't hesitate a moment. I scooped Clara into my arms and hugged her. Then I sat and bounced her on my lap and hugged her some more. Clara had waited hours for my attention, and I was happy to assure her of my love in ways she understood.

In today's psalm, David paints a picture of a God who knows our needs and delights in loving us—his children—in tangible ways. But we don't have to wait our turn; God can love the whole world at once! God's unfailing love is so immeasurable, and it extends to the heavens (v. 5). Because he loves us, he provides a protective place of refuge under his wings (v. 7) and supplies an abundant feast and drink from his river of delights (v. 8). He also gives us life and light (v. 9) and offers us salvation.

When we come to God with our needs, we don't need to question his love and ask, "Do you want to hold me?" God's Word assures us of his limitless, steadfast, precious love that extends far beyond anything we can ever comprehend. And we know God holds us: *"The eternal God is your refuge, and underneath are the everlasting arms"* (Deuteronomy 33:27).

Prayer: O Lord, how precious to me is Your unfailing love! Thank You for providing a refuge for my grandchildren and me under the shadow of Your wings.

Prepare for Joy and Tears

(It's not all fun and games)

While writing this study, I often asked for prayer. I wanted God's anointing for each lesson. One week I told a prayer warrior at church, "I'm thinking of omitting the chapter on joy and tears." She began crying and said, "Don't leave out the tears." I learned that some of her grandchildren lived on another continent and she seldom saw them. Weeks later she asked, "Did you leave in the tears?"

I did, because although some moments of grandparenting are pure ecstasy, others pierce our hearts. The fun-and-games part of grandparenting is mixed with heartaches. Our sorrows come in different shapes and sizes, but all are filtered through God's loving hands and compassionate heart.

This week we'll find joy in our sorrows and comfort in our tears. We'll also discuss fun ways to celebrate with our grandchildren.

Day One	Joy in Tears
Day Two	Triumph in Trials
Day Three	Celebrate! Holidays and Ordinary Days
Day Four	Celebrate! Birthdays, Traditions, and Eternal Events
Day Five	Joy and Compassion of Jesus

Joy in Tears

I wish life on earth always ended "happily ever after." But the Bible doesn't promise problem-free lives.

Heartwork

1. John 16:33 says, *"In this world you will have trouble. But take heart! I have overcome the world."*

What does this verse promise we will have?

_____

_____

Why can we take heart during troubles?

_____

_____

2. James also writes about trials: *"Consider it pure joy, my brothers, whenever you face trials of many kinds"* (James 1:2).
How are we to view trials?

_____

_____

Since we don't live in a world of make-believe, it's not a matter of *if* we will have trials but *when.* Everyone experiences trials, and some spill over into grandparenting.

Kerri sat in my burgundy rocker, crying inconsolably. "I finally have a granddaughter, and now my missionary kids are moving to India. I'll seldom see them."

Marla's son and daughter-in-law had six miscarriages. Finally her daughter-in-law carried the baby full-term, only to deliver him stillborn.

When my friend Dottie called, I expected news of their first grandchild's birth. Instead I learned their son, the father of their grandchild-to-be, had unexpectedly died. What a shock!

Shortly before Christmas, we learned our fourteen-month-old grandson had holes in his heart and needed surgery. Suddenly Christmas lost its glitter.

In some cases, grandparents' hearts are broken because their children divorce and leave less-than-ideal situations for their grandchildren. Other grandparents feel sorrow because their grandchildren are abused, neglected, or raised in ungodly homes. Some situations are too horrendous to mention. And, if parents are incapable of caring for their children, grandparents may have to raise them. Also, sickness keeps some grandparents from feeling *grand* enough to grandparent.

> May the God of hope fill you with all joy and peace as you trust in him, so that you may overflow with hope by the power of the Holy Spirit. (Romans 15:13)

And yet James 1:2 says to count these trials as joy? I didn't feel joy when diagnosed with incurable lymphoma or when my daughter, the mother of two of my grandsons, was diagnosed with early-stage cancer. And I cried myself to sleep when our infant grandson faced surgery.

3. Read James 1:2–4 to learn why we can face trials with joy:

> *Consider it pure joy, my brothers, whenever you face trials of many kinds, because you know that the testing of your faith develops perseverance. Perseverance must finish its work so that you may be mature and complete, not lacking anything.*

List the progression from facing trials to not lacking anything.

_____

_____

_____

_____

_____

I like the outcome of trials, but not the process. When I focus only on my present life, I don't welcome trials. But when I view them from an eternal perspective, I see a glimmer of their value. And I can experience the true joy we discussed in Week 3 if I allow the Holy Spirit to produce joy in my life.

4. Have you faced, or are you presently facing, grandparenting trials? If so, how do you view these trials?

_____

_____

_____

How can God help you with your problems and your perspective about them? How can God use them for good?

_____

_____

_____

Naomi and Ruth

Let's look at the biblical account of Naomi, Ruth, and Obed, where God worked for good even through trials. The entire book of Ruth totals eighty-five verses in four short chapters. If you've never read it, treat yourself by reading the entire story in one sitting. I've included a summary and pertinent passages for this lesson. I think of Ruth as a love story with a happy ending. But it didn't start that way.

Due to a famine in Israel, Naomi, her husband, and their two sons left Israel and moved to Moab. Then Naomi's husband died, and her sons married Moabite women named Orpah and Ruth. After about ten years, both her sons died.

Talk about high stress points in life—relocating to a foreign country and three deaths! Plus, it appears she has no potential for grandchildren.

Naomi heard the famine in Israel was over, so she decided to return to her hometown, Bethlehem. Although her daughters-in-law accompanied her, Naomi told them, *"Go back, each of you, to your mother's home"* (Ruth 1:8). However, the daughters-in-law still wanted to go with her. But Naomi said, *"Return home, my daughters. . . . It is more bitter for me than for you, because the LORD's hand has gone out against me!"* (Ruth 1:11, 13).

Orpah decided to return to her people and her gods. But Ruth said, *"Don't urge me to leave you or to turn back from you. Where you go I will go, and where you stay I will stay. Your people will be my people and your God my God"* (Ruth 1:16).

I admire Ruth's loyalty and commitment to Naomi and her God.

> *I remember months of caring for my daughter during her bed rest. Since she was forty and considered old for pregnancy, we worried about the baby being okay. Everything turned out fine, and God created a special boy, who is now five. Although I may not live to see what God does in his adult life, I know He has wonderful plans for my grandson's future."* Grandma Erna

5. From the story so far, begin filling in the first two columns below with Naomi's and Ruth's character traits and trials. We'll add more as the story continues.

	Character Traits	Tears and Trials	Joy and Blessings
Naomi			
Ruth			

So the two women went on until they came to Bethlehem. When they arrived in Bethlehem, the whole town was stirred because of them, and the women exclaimed, "Can this be Naomi?" "Don't call me Naomi," she told them. "Call me Mara, because the Almighty has made my life very bitter. I went away full, but the LORD has brought me back empty." (Ruth 1:19–21)

Naomi means "pleasant" and *Mara* means "bitter." Naomi now calls herself "bitter." When we face difficulties, we can either become bitter or better. Hebrews 12:15 warns against becoming bitter: *"See to it that no one misses the grace of God and that no bitter root grows up to cause trouble and defile many."*

> **Ruth means "friend."**

But their story isn't over. *"Ruth the Moabitess said to Naomi, 'Let me go to the fields and pick up the leftover grain behind anyone in whose eyes I find favor'"* (Ruth 2:2).

It turned out Ruth gleaned in the field of Boaz, a distant relative of Elimelech, Naomi's deceased husband. When Boaz learned who Ruth was, he instructed the workers to leave barley for her.

Boaz said to Ruth:

> *"I've been told all about what you have done for your mother-in-law since the death of your husband—how you left your father and mother and your homeland and came to live with a people you did not know before. May the LORD repay you for what you have done. May you be richly rewarded by the LORD, the God of Israel, under whose wings you have come to take refuge."* (Ruth 2:11, 12)

> **Even though Naomi was not the biological mother of Ruth or Boaz, in her culture, she was considered a grandmother. And Obed was considered to be her son's child and would receive the family inheritance.**

6. Add to the chart about Naomi and Ruth, and about God's blessings to them.

As the story continues, Naomi helps a romance blossom between Ruth and Boaz. They marry, Ruth gives birth to a son named Obed, and Naomi in some respects becomes a grandmother!

> *The women said to Naomi: "Praise be to the LORD, who this day has not left you without a kinsman-redeemer. May he become famous throughout Israel! He will renew your life and sustain you in your old age. For your daughter-in-law, who loves you and who is better to you than seven sons, has given him birth."* (Ruth 4:14, 15)

What a favorable reputation Ruth had among those who observed her! And what a beautiful picture of how grandson Obed could bless Naomi.

7. In the chart, continue to fill in more character traits of Naomi and Ruth, and the blessings they received from God.

Did the women's prediction of Obed becoming famous come true? Obed became the father of Jesse and the grandfather of David, the greatest king in Israel. Not only that, you'll find Obed listed in the lineage of Christ. *"Boaz the father of Obed, whose mother was Ruth, Obed the father of Jesse, and Jesse the father of King David"* (Matthew 1:5, 6).

Ruth became the great-grandmother of King David and was also listed in the kingly line of Jesus the Messiah. Boaz's wish came true: *"May the LORD repay you for what you have done. May you be richly rewarded by the LORD"* (Ruth 2:12). What a story of finding joy in tears!

8. *"Then Naomi took the child, laid him in her lap and cared for him"* (Ruth 4:16). What qualities did Naomi possess that made her a wonderful grandmother? (See the chart for her character traits.)

_____

_____

_____

9. What grandparenting lessons of hope and joy can we learn and apply from Naomi's life?

_____

_____

_____

GRAND Thought: Whatever sorrow you face, realize it is not the end of the story. God can bring hope and beauty from dark situations. But often it takes time to find joy in tears. Lean close to God, and trust Him as you wait.

Y*ou always hope your children and grandchildren will have a life free of heartache, but life is real. So you pray, you trust God to straighten out the messes in life, you rejoice before you see anything happening, and you rejoice again when God works through impossible situations. Sometimes it takes a long time, but praise God, He is faithful."*
Grandma Barbara

Prayer: Almighty God, thank You for the story of Ruth, which shows Your love, provision, and power in difficulties. With You, there's hope in hopeless situations. With You, all things are possible. You can redeem any difficulty. So we lay our burdens down at Your feet. And while we wait for You to work in our children's and grandchildren's lives, please replace our tears with joy and help us trust You more.

(Based on Matthew 19:26)

Triumph in Trials

Day Two

As I drove home from an evening meeting, my thoughts were on Owen, our sixteen-month-old grandson who was facing open-heart surgery soon. The previous week I had accompanied our son and his wife as they met with the surgeon, so I knew the grim details. "We'll stop his heart and put him on a heart and lung machine," the surgeon said. One question nagged me: *What if he dies?*

I turned on the radio, hoping to find soothing music to comfort my anxious heart. Instrumental strains of "I Surrender All" played and reminded me of the words in the song: "*All* to Him I freely give."

"Oh, no, Lord! I have to give you Owen!" I sobbed in response.

At that moment, I realized I hadn't fully relinquished my grandson. I had tried to place him in God's hands, but I still clutched him tightly. I cried the rest of the way home as I struggled to surrender Owen to the Lord.

Later, I wrote these words as a prayer of relinquishment:

> Jesus, take this little lamb,
> I place him gently in Your hand.
> Make his heart and body whole,
> Let him praise You heart and soul.
>
> Jesus, take this little lamb,
> I place him safely in Your hand.
> He always was and will be Yours,
> Thank you for the time he's ours.

Heartwork

You may not have a grandson who needs heart surgery, but you may have other heartaches. Most of us don't skip through life without problems. In the playground of life, we can't ride the merry-go-round forever. Sometimes the *merry* is gone and we just go 'round and 'round. Often life seems more like a teeter-totter, with ups and downs. But God doesn't leave us to muddle through our difficulties alone. He's right there with us. He sees our tears and hears our sobs as we cry out to Him.

> Out of the depths I cry to you, O LORD. (Psalm 130:1)

1. According to Psalm 56:8, what does God do with our sorrows and tears?

> *You keep track of all my sorrows. You have collected all my tears in your bottle. You have recorded each one in your book.* (NLT)

_____

How precious to know that God values our tears! He must have a large bottle for all mine!

2. It shouldn't surprise us that Jesus cares about our grief. Underline the words in Isaiah 53:3 that describe His grief:

> *"He was despised and rejected by men, a man of sorrows, and familiar with suffering."*

Since Jesus experienced sorrow and suffering, He knows how to comfort us. As I awoke one morning a few weeks before Owen's surgery, God put the words of Hebrews 12:2 in my mind: *"Let us fix our eyes on Jesus, the author and perfecter of our faith, who for the joy set before him endured the cross."*

I knew God wanted me to understand and apply this verse.

3. Read Hebrews 12:2 again. What principles can you find to apply when facing trials?

_____

_____

_____

The verse begins by telling us to *"fix our eyes on Jesus,"* and that's the place to start. But the main words I noticed were *joy* and *endured*. As I read Hebrews 12:3, I found the word *endured* again. *"Consider him who endured such opposition from sinful men, so that you will not grow weary and lose heart."* Jesus is our example, and He endured pain and sorrow.

Before Owen's surgery and during his recovery, God reminded me that some seasons are times to *endure*. We just need to get through them. They aren't pleasant, so we wait them out. But we also look forward to the *joy* ahead—because, no matter how difficult the situation, there *will* be joy later. With Owen, I put my thoughts on fast-forward to the joy that would come—for Owen's heart to be healed either on earth or in heaven.

4. Look again at Hebrews 12:2, 3. What did Jesus endure? What was the joy He looked forward to?

Jesus endured   Joy ahead

_____   _____

_____   _____

_____   _____

Part of His joy was knowing that His *death* would bring us eternal *life!*

5. Perhaps you're in the middle of a hard grandparenting situation now. If so, identify the trial and the future joy.

Trial to endure   Joy ahead

_____   _____

_____   _____

_____   _____

From our grandbabies' first cries at birth, we find that life mingles joy and tears. Although we might plan all joy for them, our grandchildren are God's, not ours, and their lives are in His hands. He has numbered their days and knows what each of those days will include. Although we were surprised to learn Owen needed heart surgery, God wasn't. Nothing that touches our grandchildren or us takes Him by surprise. *"All the days ordained for me were written in your book before one of them came to be"* (Psalm 139:16).

As I watched my grandson cry inconsolably after surgery, I

wept, too. It was a time to endure. But three years later, there's joy! Looking at my energetic grandson, I thank God for His blessing. I'm glad He planned more days for Owen!

For Grandma Kerri, who sorrowed to see her children and granddaughter leave for India as missionaries, she now rejoices in her family's spiritual impact. She misses them, but they will return home for six months to finalize the adoption of their Ethiopian daughter.

After Marla's son and daughter-in-law grieved over many childbearing losses, they gave birth to a healthy, full-term baby girl.

Grandma Dot's first grandchild, born soon after Dottie's son died, grew up in a home with a loving, Christian stepfather. She is now married and has three children of her own.

> Weeping may remain for a night, but rejoicing comes in the morning. (Psalm 30:5)

We have no guarantees that life on earth will turn out as we desire, but we know God is working for our good and His glory—and joy lies ahead.

But while we wait and endure, here are six ways God helped me take heart during adversity, written in an acrostic for TRIALS.

In the chart below, God's attributes come first, followed by your response in the second column. The verses in the third column include biblical truths about God and how we can respond to trials. The final column lists a question to help you apply the principles. You'll find space to answer the questions on the following pages under question 6.

Truths to Triumph over Trials

God's Attributes **God is:**	Actions, Attitudes **My response**	Verses	Apply
Trustworthy	**T**hankfulness	*Praise the LORD, O my soul, and forget not all his benefits.* (Psalm 103:2)	What can you thank God for today?
Reliable	**R**emember	*This I recall to my mind, therefore have I hope. It is of the LORD's mercies that we are not consumed, because his compassions fail not. They are new every morning: great is thy faithfulness.* (Lamentations 3:21–23 KJV)	How has God been faithful in the past?
Invisible but involved	**I**ntercede	*God is our refuge and strength, an ever-present help in trouble.* (Psalm 46:1) *'Call to me and I will answer you.'* (Jeremiah 33:3)	For whom can you pray? How do you need God's help?
All-knowing	**A**ccept	*O LORD, you have searched me and you know me. You are familiar with all my ways.* (Psalm 139:1, 3) *"Take this cup from me. Yet not what I will, but what you will."* (Mark 14:36)	In what area(s) do you need to leave the future in God's hands or give Him authority in your life?
Love	**L**augh	*God is love.* (1 John 4:16) *She can laugh at the days to come.* (Proverbs 31:25)	How can you add humor and laughter to your life?
Sovereign (in control)	**S**earch **S**cripture	*"For I know the plans I have for you," declares the LORD, "plans to prosper you and not to harm you, plans to give you hope and a future."* (Jeremiah 29:11)	What Bible promises can you claim?

6. Here are ways I applied these principles during trials. Add ways you can apply them.

Thankfulness

Before getting up, I thank God for another day of life. Throughout the day, I look for blessings. God's benefits may come as a cheery e-mail, a pretty flower in my yard, or even my husband washing dishes. A thankful heart helps me maintain a positive outlook during challenges. Even during the hardest times, we can thank God for life and His trustworthiness.

I'm thankful for:

_____

_____

_____

Remember

God has shown His love and compassion to our family during hard times. Sometimes I journal what God has done so I can reread these entries later. Recalling God's *past* faithfulness helps me trust Him in the present. Journaling also leaves a written record of His goodness for others to read.

I can see God's fingerprints of faithfulness in my life in:

_____

_____

_____

Intercede

We touch God's heart and impact lives through prayer. Intercession allows us to pray for others, not only for ourselves. Even during personal trials, we can fulfill the command to *"pray continually"* (1 Thessalonians 5:17). For example, when someone e-mails a concern, I often e-mail a prayer back.

> Come near to God and he will come near to you. (James 4:8)

Lord, today I pray for _____

_____

_____

Accept

Do we accept the difficulties God allows in our lives or balk at them? I wouldn't have written my life story with trials, but God included these chapters. I choose to accept them and seek to triumph over them with His help.

Lord, help me accept Your authority in my life as I face the following challenge:

_____

_____

In what area do you need to leave the future in God's hands?

_____

Laugh

It's important to add humor to our lives through books, DVDs, and cheerful friends. Studies show that laughter is therapeutic. The Bible substantiates this: *"A cheerful heart is good medicine"* (Proverbs 17:22). As we sprinkle humor into our lives, it lifts our spirits and others', even though life isn't always funny.

> To laugh in the face of adversity means you acknowledge that God is in control.

What can you do to brighten your day or someone else's?

_____

Search the Scripture

God's Word comforts and guides us. As we read the Bible, certain verses may stand out as promises or assurance. God gave me Proverbs 9:11 when I became ill: *"For through me your days will be many, and years will be added to your life."* My daughter printed and framed this verse to encourage me. It hangs in a prominent place, reminding me of God's promise.

If you don't have a special verse to encourage you during hard times, ask God to give you one. Then write it out and keep it in a visible spot.

Write a special verse that encourages you.

_____

_____

_____

_____

God promises to go before us: *"I will go before you and will level the mountains"* (Isaiah 45:2). Whenever we come to a new day or a new problem, God is already there.

> But let all who take refuge in you be glad; let them ever sing for joy. Spread your protection over them, that those who love your name may rejoice in you. For surely, O LORD, you bless the righteous; you surround them with your favor as with a shield. (Psalm 5:11, 12)

GRAND Thought: Take heart—God has promised, *"Those who sow in tears will reap with songs of joy"* (Psalm 126:5). So anticipate a harvest of joy.

Prayer: Dear Father, thank You for walking with me during hard times. As the Man of Sorrows, You understand my grief, and care deeply about my tears. Just as I run to hug my grandchildren and comfort them when they cry, so You hold me close to Your heart and comfort me. Even when circumstances don't go the way I would choose, I know You are working according to Your sovereign plan. Help me surrender my plans to You and trust You to work in my heartaches. Today, I give You my concern about _____. Please work for my good and for Your glory in it. Thank You for my eternal hope that someday You will wipe away *all* my tears, and I'll be forever with You.

> He will wipe every tear from their eyes. There will be no more death or mourning or crying or pain, for the old order of things has passed away.
> (Revelation 21:4)

Day Three

Celebrate! Holidays and Ordinary Days

Before Easter our grandkids came for a Cousins' Day. I made plans for them to act out Jesus' triumphal entry, dye eggs, and make hot cross buns.

Making the buns went smoothly. Then it was time to act out Palm Sunday. I had pruned ferns to use as palm branches. The grandchildren could take turns playing Jesus, riding down the sloped yard on the toy motorcycle, while others waved ferns and shouted, "Hosanna!"

When our oldest grandson, Peter, played Jesus, the younger grandkids half-heartedly waved their ferns, and then Clara yelled, "Let's get Peter!" The chase began to catch "Jesus."

I laughed as I watched them but thought, *This isn't what I had planned or what was in the Bible.* But, maybe it was more realistic than I realized, because in less than a week after Jesus' entry, the crowds no longer honored Him. They, too, were saying, "Let's get Him!"

When we dyed eggs, our three-year-old grandson really got into it—literally—and left with multicolored hands. We all had fun, but perhaps he had the best time.

Heartwork

Celebrations and festivals abound in the Bible. The NIV Bible uses the word *celebrate* sixty-seven times. In the Old Testament we read how the Jews celebrated Passover and other feasts that lasted days. In the New Testament, we read about the party with the fatted calf that celebrated the prodigal's homecoming. So, there's precedence to rejoice!

Today, in the spirit of rejoicing, we'll have a "snow day" with no school (Bible study). Instead I'll share a blizzard of ideas to build memories with our grandkids. Get ready for a happy romp as we discuss the fun-and-games part of grandparenting. We'll use the word CELEBRATE as an acrostic to list ideas for celebrating:

Christmas
Easter
Love
Everyday Events
Birthdays
Reunions
Accomplishments
Traditions and Trips
Eternal Events

Choose ideas that suit you and your grandkids, and put a check mark by those you'd like to try soon. Save other ideas for appropriate seasons or stages of life. Let God's Spirit direct you, and use Colossians 3:17 as a guideline: *"And whatever you do, whether in word or deed, do it all in the name of the Lord Jesus, giving thanks to God the Father through him."*

C: Christmas

Children love Christmas! Although commercialism has changed the focus from the true meaning, don't let that rob you of the joy of celebrating Jesus' birth.

Advent

Advent keeps the focus on Jesus. As grandparents expectantly await their grandchild's birth, so Advent activities help us anticipate Jesus' birth.

Make or buy an Advent wreath and purchase an Advent Scripture booklet or find suggested readings online. On each of the four Sundays before Christmas, light candles (lighting one the first week and adding one each week), read Scripture, sing carols, and pray. You could also include a snack. On Christmas, light the four candles plus the additional one in the center. If your grandchildren live far away, mail them an Advent wreath and Scripture passages. Then celebrate together across the miles as they read the same verses you do.

Birthday Gift for Jesus

Consider gifts from the heart (to be kinder, to pray more) or monetary gifts to the needy. Young children can bring toys to the church nursery, or families can support a ministry. You could give individual gifts, a family gift, or plan one you and your grandchild can give together.

> *Christmas at Grandma's house focused on Jesus, not presents. My best memories are all the grandchildren sitting on the floor around Grandma's chair as she read the Christmas story and asked us questions." Lori, age 56*

Christmas Story

Use age-appropriate Bibles or storybooks. Little ones enjoy it more with pictures. Christmas cards tell the story and can become a wall hanging—manger, shepherds, angels, and wise men, glued to a wide ribbon. With older grandchildren, families could memorize the story in Luke 2 and recite it.

Bring the story to life with drama. Grandma Ruth sewed simple costumes, and her grandchildren dressed up as nativity characters and acted out the story. Dramatizing the story internalizes Scripture in a way they'll remember.

It's our tradition to tell the Christmas story in a mixed-up way so the grandkids can correct us. I mount Christmas cards on chopsticks and print *stop* on the back of each card. Everyone gets a sign. Then as I tell the story, they hold up their "stop signs" whenever I say something incorrect. I begin, "Once upon a time," and they stop me, since this isn't a fairy tale. I continue with wrong details. The grandkids listen carefully to catch mistakes, and there's lots of laughter.

Baking

Our grandkids come over for a cookie-baking day in December. To keep the focus on Jesus, we bake sugar cookies in the shape of Nativity characters and use them to tell the Christmas story. Then each grand-child takes home a plate of decorated cookies.

A "Silent Night"

Take a walk with your grandkids under the starlit sky and talk about the star of the East. Sing "Silent Night" together and come home to hot chocolate with candy-cane stirrers. Or take a pajama ride to see neighborhood Christmas lights and talk about Jesus, the Light of the world.

Grandkids like fun and laughter. Add humor to their lives by telling funny stories and jokes. Our three-year-old grandson loved to say "I make a joke" after he said something funny. Cultivate their sense of humor and yours.

E: Easter

At Easter we celebrate Jesus' victory over death! He redeemed us!

Christmas Tree Cross

Save your Christmas tree trunk for Easter. Cut off the upper one-third and fasten it to the lower part with a nail or wire to make a cross. Leave the cross plain, decorate it, or drape it with purple fabric and add a crown of thorns. Place it in a visible spot in your home as a reminder that Jesus came to die.

Easter Cards

If your grandkids enjoy crafts, make cards. Fold colored paper in half, then cut out a cross that is hinged on the left. Decorate it and include the verse: *"I am the resurrection and the life. He who believes in me will live, even though he dies; . . . Do you believe this?"* (John 11:25, 26).

If your grandchildren live far away, send them homemade or purchased Easter cards.

My grandmother lived in Alaska, so I only met her five times in my life. But she was always sweet and kind. We corresponded throughout the years. She never forgot Christmas or birthdays, and she made me feel special. I think of her with love and see her kind eyes and smile in my mind."
Bonnie

Books and Symbols

Purchase Easter books and Resurrection Eggs for your grandchildren and yourself. Grandchildren enjoy opening these plastic eggs with symbols inside that tell the Easter story.

Food Traditions

Our grandkids enjoy eating Empty-Tomb Buns on Easter morning. Make them with biscuit dough wrapped around a large marshmallow. The marshmallow melts, leaving a sweet, empty center. Or cut a doughnut in half and stand it up to represent a tomb. A donut hole set in front becomes the stone to roll away.

L: Love

God is love, and He gives us love for our grandchildren. *"And so we know and rely on the love God has for us. God is love. Whoever lives in love lives in God, and God in him"* (1 John 4:16).

Valentine's Day

Whether your grandchildren live near or far, this is a natural time to express love. Consider sending a card, gift, money, or photo. Also include verses about God's love. My grandkids like to bake and frost heart-shaped cookies with me. If they can't come over, sometimes I mail them cookies.

Marriage and Anniversaries

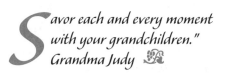
Savor each and every moment with your grandchildren."
Grandma Judy

When my husband and I reached our fortieth anniversary, we planned a party. We wanted our grandchildren to know we valued our marriage. Our bridal party attended, the grandkids sang "Jesus Loves Me," and our oldest grandson read from our wedding Bible. Our daughter told our "love story," and we listened to our taped wedding vows.

E: Everyday Events

You don't need an official holiday to celebrate. Make ordinary days extraordinary by adding something special.

First Snowfall

Make "sleds" for breakfast when it snows. French toast or pancakes are the sleds, and bacon or sausage links become the runners. Sprinkle on powdered sugar "snow."

Mealtimes

Make meals special by setting a pretty table with a centerpiece. In the summer, enjoy a spontaneous picnic or snack outside. In the winter, serve a simple meal in front of the fireplace.

Time with Grandkids

Great-Grandparents Joe and Margaret spent every Wednesday with their grandson for years. They fed ducks, shared picnics, went swimming, hiked, made up hilarious stories, watched trains, inspected construction sites, groomed dogs, and the list continues. Ordinary things can be fun!

I keep colored envelopes handy with ideas for things to do at Grandma's house. Clara likes to open her pink envelope and select an activity, such as play a game, cook, or sew.

After Grandma Kathy took her six-year-old granddaughter for a fish-and-chips lunch and a walk along the marina, her granddaughter said, "This was the best day of my whole life." What we consider insignificant can mean much to our grandkids.

> Grandkids help us see life through the eyes of a child, so we don't have to grow up!

Grandkids' Appreciation Time

Surprise your grandkids with an unexpected party. Place a welcome sign on the front door that says "Grandkids' Appreciation Party." Prepare their favorite foods, put party favors by their places, and write notes that say why you appreciate them.

Seize the moment! Every day is a special day, and life is a gift from God.

What everyday events can you turn into special occasions and fun?

Now we'll hit the pause button and CELEBRATE again tomorrow. Another "snow day!"

> *"Celebrate silliness. Don't take life too seriously. We're not too sophisticated to have fun!"* Great-Grandma Margaret 🌸

GRAND Thought: It's easy to get caught up in the busyness of life and miss the fun and joy of daily living. The Bible tells us God gives us everything we need to enJOY life.

Prayer: Heavenly Father, thank You for my grandchildren and the joy they bring. They are truly precious gifts from You. Help me enjoy them and celebrate with them now, because they'll grow up fast. When they aren't nearby, give me creative ideas to show my love from a distance. And when they're nearby, may Your love and gracious Spirit overflow from me to them. Help me lighten up and share fun and laughter with them. Thank You that You rejoice over them with singing. Show me ways to make them feel special and rejoice *with* them and *over* them.

(Based on Zephaniah 3:17)

> Trust . . . in the living God, who gives us richly all things to enjoy. (1 Timothy 6:17 NKJV)

Day Four

Celebrate! Birthdays, Traditions, and Eternal Events

Let's continue to cele**brate** as we focus on:

C
E
L
E
Birthdays
Reunions
Accomplishments
Traditions and Trips
Eternal Events

"This is the day the LORD has made; let us rejoice and be glad in it" (Psalm 118:24).

Choose ideas that work for you.

B: Birthdays

Make Them Memorable

"I don't have *quantity* time with my grandchildren, but I try to make their birthdays special. For one granddaughter, I purchased a birthday keepsake plate that party guests signed." Grandma Nan

"I sewed a quilt for my granddaughter's eighteenth birthday. Then we traveled six hours to deliver the quilt and help her celebrate." Grandma Dianna

"I have twenty-four grandchildren, and I buy all of them birthday gifts. I shop at secondhand stores year-round. I love to remember them on their special days." Grandma Donna

> If one member is honored, all the members rejoice with it.
> (1 Corinthians 12:26 NKJV)

Add Spiritual Touches

My husband and I select presents from the grandkids' wish lists and also include a spiritual gift, such as a Christian storybook or an age-appropriate Bible. We write Bible verses in their cards.

A gift of prayer makes a lasting birthday gift. Sometimes my husband Milt and I set aside an hour to pray for our birthday child. Then we send a note telling the grandchild what we prayed for them.

Some birthdays I write a poem about my grandchild's life based on God's Word, then I read it at the family party. Here's part of the "Ode to Owen" I wrote based on Psalm 139:

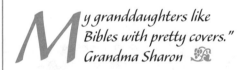

My granddaughters like Bibles with pretty covers."
Grandma Sharon

> God saw Owen before he was born.
>   Owen, you're two and we love you!
> He made each part of his cute little form.
>   Owen, you're two and we love you!

Share Photos and Birth Stories

Grandkids love to hear stories about their birth or adoption and their importance to us. Tell them God has a special plan for them and you're glad they are part of your family. If your grandchildren live far away, write their birth stories in a card. Or make an audio or video recording of your message and mail it. Include pictures.

Use framed pictures of the birthday grandchild as the table centerpiece. Also make birthday cards from photocopied pictures.

> For you created my inmost being; you knit me together in my mother's womb. (Psalm 139:13)

Our grandchildren will remember *how we made them feel* much longer than *what we gave them.*

1. How can you make your grandchildren's birthdays special? What would they enjoy?

_____

_____

_____

R: Reunions

Extended Family

Every few years my extended family of siblings, their children, and their grandchildren gather for several days. We include fun intergenerational activities but also share our faith and pray together. Members of the oldest generation draw names of children in the youngest generation, and these two become prayer partners at the reunion, and for months to follow. That's how my grade-school-aged grandson got to know my oldest brother, who is in his eighties. And during the time my husband was praying for one niece's daughter after the reunion, she became a Christian. If your family doesn't hold reunions, draw names at Christmas and pray for each other until Easter.

> There, in the presence of the LORD your God, you and your families shall eat and shall rejoice in everything you have put your hand to, because the LORD your God has blessed you.
> Deuteronomy 12:7

Our family also holds mini-reunions when relatives come to town. One time we used Psalm 136 as a litany of thanksgiving and recounted ways God had blessed our extended family. The young grandkids danced around and waved paper banners while repeating the line, "His love endures forever."

Immediate Family

We plan special events for our grandkids several times a year, and call it Cousins' Day. Sometimes we attend a children's play, cook favorite foods, or draw names and become secret cousins for the day.

When Grandma Petey's grandchildren gather, she plans special projects, such as making stepping-stones for the garden. She also saves her grandchildren's schoolwork, poetry, and stories, and compiles them into a book for each grandchild, which she prints at the copy center.

Some grandparents host a weeklong Grand Camp or Cousins' Camp for their grandkids. Building family relationships takes time, energy, and prayer. But it's worth it!

*T*reasure hunts and playing hide-and-seek in the dark with flashlights are fun any time.

2. What ideas do you have for special gatherings with your family?

_____

_____

_____

> Lord, you have been our dwelling place throughout all generations.
> (Psalm 90:1)

A: Accomplishments

Life is too short *not* to celebrate milestones. Milestones can be as small as your grandchild learning to tie a shoe or as large as graduating from college. Any accomplishment can be a reason to celebrate in simple or lavish ways.

Back-to-School and School Year-End

Celebrate new beginnings before school starts. Sometimes we invite our grandchildren for a day of back-to-school shopping and fun. They choose where to eat and help select new clothes.

The end of the school year marks moving up another grade and perhaps changing schools. Grandma Dianna said, "On the last day (of school), we always celebrate with the grandkids. We go out to lunch, or sometimes just have Ding Dongs as a celebration." If your grandkids don't live nearby, you could call, e-mail, send a card, congratulate them with a gift, or pray for God's blessing in their lives.

Significant Milestones

Graduations and new careers are certainly reasons to celebrate. Grandma Barbara says of her adult grandchildren, "No matter their age, it's pure joy to watch them stretch their wings and fly. You pray they don't crash and get hurt, but it's an exciting time." Soon Barbara will celebrate one grandson's doctoral degree, and she rejoices to see another wear his white doctor's coat.

Celebrate God's Will

Some events are especially important to our kids and grandkids. They may want to win a school election, make the basketball team, or earn a special award.

> *If you can't celebrate with your grandchildren, send cards to congratulate them. Remind them God gifted them, and that you're pleased they are using their talents.*

When our daughter auditioned for a school musical, I wanted her to get an important part. As I struggled, asking God to give her the lead role, I realized what I really wanted was God's will. So I planned a special dinner to celebrate God's will—win or lose. Other times, we celebrated God's will even before we knew the outcome.

When our grandchildren are involved in competitions and elections, celebrating wins *or* losses adds joy to winning or helps take the sting out of losing. Also, celebrating God's will emphasizes He is sovereign and knows what is best.

3. List three upcoming family milestones. How can you honor these accomplishments?

> For you have been my hope, O Sovereign LORD, my confidence since my youth. (Psalm 71:5)

_____

_____

_____

_____

_____

_____

T: Traditions and Trips

It doesn't take long for grandkids to consider something as a tradition (and that's a compliment). Be careful what you start!

Traditions

Traditions are often centered around holidays and usually include special foods and activities. On Thanksgiving weekend, Grandma Cheryl invites her children and grandchildren to come for dinner and to help get out her large nutcracker collection.

Years ago, we started taking our children and grandchildren for an overnight to see the Lights of Christmas. We all look forward to this annual tradition.

Grandparents Bill and Ruth vacationed with their family at Priest Lake, Idaho, when their kids were young. Now, with married children and grandchildren, they still do. At Bill and Ruth's fiftieth anniversary party, numerous photos showed them making fun memories with their grandkids while vacationing together.

Traditions (and trips) don't need to be expensive. Plan ones that suit your budget. Your grandchildren will remember the time shared and the love they felt, not what you spent.

Trips

For young grandkids, plan short trips close to home, and let the parents and grandkids help plan them.

Grandma Beryl took her grandkids on a train trip and stayed overnight in a hotel. They have also traced the Lewis and Clark trail and camped together for a week. After their trips, Beryl creates memory books with photos and write-ups about their adventures.

Grandma Nan shared, "When a grandchild turns thirteen, I take him or her on a memorable trip for two or three weeks. It's just the two of us sharing thoughts, ideas, and spiritual things, and making lasting memories."

John and Nina's grandkids (ages four to ten) were eager to visit Disneyland again. But they didn't think they would get another chance.

One day the four grandkids and their parents came to Grandpa and Grandma's home to supposedly make a video. When the kids were asked to talk about favorite vacations on the video, Disneyland came up. Just then Grandpa John appeared from the bedroom wearing a Goofy hat. "Did someone say Disneyland?" he asked. "I'd like to go."

"Okay," Grandma Nina said and smiled. "Let's go right now!"

The grandkids thought they were joking, until their grandparents brought out their packed suitcases.

"We're ready to go," said Grandma Nina.

"We can't pack that fast," said one of the grandkids.

"You don't need to," her mother said. "Our suitcases are packed and in the car."

When the kids realized the trip was for real, they went berserk!

Everyone had a wonderful time at Disneyland. And Grandpa John is probably still chuckling about pulling off that surprise—even though he's in heaven now. The family is so glad they had that special time with him before he died. Create memories and celebrate while you can.

4. What ideas do you have for traditions or trips with your grandchildren?

_____

_____

_____

E: Eternal Events

Spiritual Birthdays

Once a year we celebrate all our grandchildren's spiritual birthdays together. We included Owen, even when he was too young to have one yet. But while I wrote this study, Owen became a Christian, too!

One time we used a royal theme and the grandkids wore paper crowns that said "King Jesus." I prepared their chairs at the table with puffy pillows and fringed blankets. Place settings included their framed pictures, and we

> I have no greater joy than to hear that my children are walking in the truth. (3 John 1:4)

served royal foods, like tortilla crowns and chocolate-dipped pretzel scepters. It was quite a regal event!

Since it's a *birthday* party, we include gifts. For the royal-themed party I placed a large treasure chest in the backyard, and they followed clues to find gifts marked for Prince Alex, Princess Clara, and the others. Each of them also received a felt bookmark with the date of their spiritual birthday.

> My lips will shout for joy when I sing praise to you—I, whom you have redeemed. (Psalm 71:23)

5. What spiritual events can you celebrate with your grandchildren? How can you nurture their spiritual growth?

_____

_____

_____

GRAND Thought: Fun doesn't *just happen*. Be intentional about celebrating. Plan ways to create lasting memories with your grandchildren. They'll talk about the "remember when" times long after you're gone.

Prayer: Heavenly Father, thank You for the joy of grandparenting. Show me fresh ways to celebrate and to make memories with my grandchildren—ways tailor-made for them. You created them and know all about them. As I spend time with them, may Your joy be my strength, so I radiate Your joy to them.

(Based on Psalm 139:1, 2; Nehemiah 8:10)

Joy and Compassion of Jesus

Day Five

When we gathered for our grandson Owen's fourth birthday party, his mother said, "I want Owen to open this gift first." After Owen ripped it open, she smiled and held a T-shirt in front of him that said, "I'm going to be a big brother!" Another grandbaby? We all clapped and cheered at this unexpected announcement. Owen's "Happy Birthday" had just become happier.

Owen was excited about the baby, too. In fact, the next morning he asked, "Where's the baby?"

I chuckled when I heard Owen expected his "gift" immediately. But this baby, our fifth grandchild, is not only a gift for Owen. All the family joyfully anticipates this child's arrival. And it seems appropriate that our grandchild's due date is about the same time as this grandparenting Bible study is expected to be released.

Heartwork

What could bring more joy than the birth of a baby? One of my favorite Bible passages tells how prophecy was fulfilled with a long-expected baby—Jesus. Luke, chapter 2, introduces Simeon and Anna, two elderly people who waited much longer than nine months for Jesus' birth and the joy He would bring.

Let me set the scene. As the law required, Mary and Joseph came to the temple in Jerusalem to consecrate their six-week-old son, Jesus. While there, two prophetic messengers approached them.

1. As you read this Luke passage, underline the character traits of Simeon and Anna.

Simeon's Song

Now there was a man in Jerusalem called Simeon, who was righteous and devout. He was waiting for the consolation of Israel, and the Holy Spirit was upon him. It had been revealed to him by the Holy Spirit that he would not die before he had seen the Lord's Christ. Moved by the Spirit, he went into the temple courts. When the parents brought in the child Jesus to do for him what the custom of the Law required, Simeon took him in his arms and praised God, saying:

> *"Sovereign Lord, as you have promised,*
> *you now dismiss your servant in peace.*
> *For my eyes have seen your salvation,*
> *which you have prepared in the sight of all people,*
> *a light for revelation to the Gentiles*
> *and for glory to your people Israel."*

The child's father and mother marveled at what was said about him. Then Simeon blessed them and said to

Mary, his mother: "This child is destined to cause the falling and rising of many in Israel, and to be a sign that will be spoken against, so that the thoughts of many hearts will be revealed. And a sword will pierce your own soul too." (Luke 2:25–35)

What a hard prophecy for a mother to hear! It certainly combines joy and tears.

Anna's Announcement

There was also a prophetess, Anna, the daughter of Phanuel, of the tribe of Asher. She was very old; she had lived with her husband seven years after her marriage, and then was a widow until she was eighty-four. She never left the temple but worshiped night and day, fasting and praying. Coming up to them at that very moment, she gave thanks to God and spoke about the child to all who were looking forward to the redemption of Jerusalem. (Luke 2:36–38)

In church I held my great-grandson, Cole, who is four months old. He is a contented cuddler. During the singing, he watched me closely and then began to sing also—too sweet!" Great-Grandma Margaret

2. Record the traits you underlined for Simeon and Anna. Then add traits not mentioned that are evident by their lives.

Simeon's Godly Character Traits	Anna's Godly Character Traits

Although Luke doesn't tell us if either Simeon or Anna had grandchildren, his description of them shows they would be good role models as grandparents.

3. Which of Simeon's and Anna's character traits would you like to model?

_____

_____

_____

I'm impressed (and convicted) by their priorities and desires. They longed to see the Messiah, who is called *"the Desire of All Nations"* (Haggai 2:7 NKJV). What is your desire? Is it Jesus, *"the Desire of All Nations"*?

These godly saints remind me of Psalm 37:4: *"Delight yourself in the LORD and he will give you the desires of your heart."* Note the verbs *delight* and *give*. Simeon and Anna delighted, and God gave.

After a lifetime of waiting for Jesus' birth, and anticipating the fulfillment of God's promise to them, Simeon and Anna saw the Messiah face-to-face. Simeon even got to hold the Promised One. What would it feel like to hold the God of the universe in your arms knowing He held you in the palm of His hand? Did Simeon's heart flutter with joy? Did tears stream down his cheeks as he praised God and blessed the baby Jesus and His family? What a wonderful climax to a life devoted to God! What a holy moment! Wouldn't you have loved to be there?

After Anna saw Jesus, she proclaimed His birth to everyone around her. I wish I could have seen her exuberance and listened to her words. God had answered her many prayers. She had experienced the highlight of her life. The long-awaited Redeemer had come!

4. Read Luke 2:25–38 again, and star the words used to describe Jesus and His purpose for coming to earth. What thoughts about Jesus stand out to you?

_____

_____

I was drawn to the sentence telling that Jesus came to be the *"consolation of Israel"* (v. 25). For me, *console* means "to comfort and show compassion." But Jesus came not only as the consolation for the Jews, He also came as *"a light for*

> *I feel such joy when my sleepy grandson wakes up in the morning and wants to rock and snuggle. We climb into my rocking chair, wrap up in a blanket, and cuddle as we begin our day. We look out the window and thank God for what we see. I know there are sorrows and hard work in grandparenting, but the joys keep me going." Grandma Erna*

revelation to the Gentiles" (v. 32). He brought salvation for *all* people. In this last lesson on joy and tears, we see that Jesus came to bring **joy** and light to a world in darkness and **tears**. And He came with **compassion** for those sorrowing. *"Return to Me with all your heart, with fasting and weeping and mourning . . . Return to the LORD your God, for He is gracious and compassionate, slow to anger and abounding in love"* (Joel 2:12, 13).

> *I*n his Christmas letter, Grandpa John broadcast this news about his grandchild: "We think our grandson is the brightest kid on the block, but that's just our unbiased opinion." 🐾

Jesus' Compassion

Let's focus on Jesus' compassion, so we can model it and show compassion to our grandchildren.

5. In these situations, underline the word that shows Jesus' motivation in his actions and teaching.

Need	Jesus' Response
Hungry crowd	*Jesus called his disciples to him and said, "I have compassion for these people; they have already been with me three days and have nothing to eat. I do not want to send them away hungry, or they may collapse on the way."* (Matthew 15:32)
Two blind men	*Jesus had compassion on them and touched their eyes. Immediately they received their sight and followed him.* (Matthew 20:34)
Man with leprosy	*Filled with compassion, Jesus reached out his hand and touched the man. "I am willing," he said. "Be clean!"* (Mark 1:41)
Prodigal son	*So he got up and went to his father. "But while he was still a long way off, his father saw him and was filled with compassion for him; he ran to his son, threw his arms around him and kissed him.* (Luke 15:20)

During His earthly ministry, Jesus acted in compassion to meet physical, emotional, and spiritual needs. He fed the hungry, healed the sick, and forgave sins. His compassion drew people to Him, and they followed Him.

Perhaps we can't heal the sick, but we can show compassion as we feed the hungry (including ravenous grandkids), pray for others, and forgive those who hurt us.

Even though Jesus no longer walks on Earth, He left us the Holy Spirit, who is also called "the Comforter." *"Nevertheless I tell you the truth; It is expedient for you that I go away: for if I go not away, the Comforter will not come unto you; but if I depart, I will send him unto you"* (John 16:7 KJV). And God's Spirit helps us show compassion.

How can we specifically show compassion?

Showing Compassion to Our Grandchildren

6. Read the story in Luke 7:11–15 to learn how Jesus showed compassion:

> *[11] Soon afterward, Jesus went to a town called Nain, and his disciples and a large crowd went along with him. [12] As he approached the town gate, a dead person was being carried out—the only son of his mother, and she was a widow. And a large crowd from the town was with her. [13] When the Lord saw her, his heart went out to her and he said, "Don't cry."*
>
> *[14] Then he went up and touched the coffin, and those carrying it stood still. He said, "Young man, I say to you, get up!" [15] The dead man sat up and began to talk, and Jesus gave him back to his mother.*

> When he saw the crowds, he had compassion on them, because they were harassed and helpless, like sheep without a shepherd.
> (Matthew 9:36)

Could anything be more heart-wrenching than the death of a child? But because of Jesus' compassion, this story had a happy ending—from tears to joy!

At a Christian conference, I heard Frank Colacurcio speak on Luke 7:11–15, and he highlighted three steps to show compassion. Like Jesus, we can:

- **See** the need. *"When the Lord saw her, his heart went out to her"* (v. 13).
- **Speak.** *"He said, 'Don't cry'"* (v. 13). Jesus planned to help.
- **Act.** *"Then he went up and touched the coffin, and those carrying it stood still. He said, 'Young man, I say to you, get up!'"* (v. 14). It takes action to help.

(Frank Colacurcio, The Firs Family Camp in Bellingham, Washington, 2002)

7. When your children and grandchildren face hard times, in which of the following ways might you respond?

_____ "I'm too busy."

_____ "I want to help."

_____ "Don't act like a baby. Just get over it!"

_____ "What a hard situation. I wish I could take away your pain."

_____ "I know you have a need, but it's not *my* problem."

_____ "I'm praying for you. What else can I do?"

_____ "I accept you no matter what happens."

_____ Other _____

8. How can you see, speak, and act to show God's heart of compassion to your grandchildren? Ask God's Spirit to direct you, and then list ideas.

_____

_____

_____

_____

GRAND Thought: Grandparenting is filled with joy and tears. During our times of tears, Jesus treats us with compassion. If we follow His example and act with compassion toward our grandchildren, they will be attracted to Jesus and us. And that brings us joy.

Prayer: Ask God to fill your heart with His joy and compassion as you pray this poem.

Honor and Praises

by Jennifer Anne F. Messing

Lord, may my countenance
glow with Your radiance.
May my smile
beam with Your joy.
May my heart
be softened
with Your compassion.
May my words
impart grace and truth.

May my presence
bring love and cheer
to family and friends.
May my whole life
bring honor and praises
to You.

Weekend Devotion

Basking in God's Love

Give thanks to the LORD, for he is good; his love endures forever. (Psalm 118:1, 29)

Read: Psalm 118:1–4, 19–29

I wanted to do something special for my grandson's second birthday. I decided to write short sentences about him, with a repeated refrain everyone could chant.

After Peter opened his gifts, it was time for the litany of love. I began, "Before the foundations of the earth, God planned for Peter's birth." Then everyone chimed in, "We love you, Peter, and we're glad you were born!" Although Peter had his back toward us and was playing with his new toys, he turned when he heard the second chorus of, "We love you, Peter, and we're glad you were born!" His grin widened as he listened. Soon he danced with glee as he heard the affirming words over and over. When we finished the last "We love you, Peter, and we're glad you were born!" he beamed and said, "Again." Even a two-year-old can't get too much love and affirmation.

God knows we also need affirmations of His love. Today's psalm assures us *"his love endures forever"* (vv. 1–4, 29). God's love is deep, and He demonstrates it beyond words. He answers us, and He is our salvation (v. 21). He does marvelous things (v. 23), saves us, grants us success (v. 25), and makes His light shine upon us (v. 27).

Just as little Peter didn't tire of hearing we loved him, we can never experience too much of God's love. Experiencing God's love evokes our grateful response. Let's join the festal procession and worship the Lord (v. 27).

Prayer: Heavenly Father, *"You are my God, and I will give you thanks; you are my God, and I will exalt you"* (v. 28). Today, I bask in Your enduring love for my grandchildren and me.

WEEK SIX

Prepare to Make an Eternal Impact

(Passing the baton of faith)

On Memorial Day weekend, Peter and Clara, our nine- and five-year-old grandkids, came for a fun afternoon with Grandpa and me. Before we took them to the beach, I decided to stop at the cemetery and visit my parents' gravesite.

I read the words engraved on my parents' stone aloud: *"As for me and my house, we will serve the LORD."* I explained that after my father died, I had asked Mother which verse she wanted on their tombstone, and she chose Joshua 24:15 (KJV). "She said, *"'Me and my house"* includes everybody.'" I continued, "Your great-grandma was thinking of you when she chose that verse. She wanted everyone in her family to love Jesus and follow Him."

Then we sat on the ground by the gravesite, bowed our heads, and thanked God for our godly heritage.

My parents weren't rich, but they passed on priceless spiritual treasures.

We've come to the most important week of this study. What lasting legacy will we leave? Let's build a strong foundation with these eternal building blocks:

Day One	Enduring Faith
Day Two	Love for God's Word
Day Three	Excitement for Prayer
Day Four	Faith Stories
Day Five	Generational Blessings

Enduring Faith

What are the most valuable possessions you have to pass on? Money, property, antiques?

Heartwork

1. *"For what will it profit a man if he gains the whole world, and loses his own soul?"* (Mark 8:36 NKJV). Based on this verse, what is most important to pass on to your family?

_____

_____

Our children and grandchildren may appreciate the temporal things we leave, and it is even biblical to do so. Proverbs 13:22 says, *"A good man leaves an inheritance for his children's children."* However, material possessions don't last.

2. Read Matthew 6:19, 20, and compare what happens to treasures on earth with what happens to those in heaven:

> *Do not store up for yourselves treasures on earth, where moth and rust destroy, and where thieves break in and steal. But store up for yourselves treasures in heaven, where moth and rust do not destroy, and where thieves do not break in and steal.*

On earth _____

In heaven _____

What if your home burned down? Or what if all your possessions were stolen? What would remain to pass on?

In contrast to earthly treasure, an eternal inheritance lasts forever—it impacts generation after generation. We can make an amazing imprint on descendants we won't meet until we're in heaven. Even now, my parents, who taught me about Jesus, have helped build faith into my children and grandchildren and generations to come. It's a ripple effect. And the ripples of their faith continue further than I can see in my lifetime.

> The house of the righteous contains great treasure. (Proverbs 15:6)

My niece Joan (age 46), one of my parents' grandchildren, shares the far-reaching effect of their enduring faith: "I remember Bible stories, biblical principles, and lessons Grandpa taught me as a child, and I've saved a journal of stories he wrote for me. His wisdom helped shape my Christian worldview and still impacts how I live my life and teach my children. What a blessing!"

Let's look at a biblical example of passing on a legacy of faith. Perhaps Lois, with her strong influence on her grandson Timothy, is the most highly regarded grandmother in the Bible. All of us have been impacted by her lasting legacy. We get a glimpse of her sincere faith as the apostle Paul writes to Timothy, whom he is mentoring as a new pastor.

3. In 2 Timothy 1:5, what three generations are mentioned and what does each one possess? Include all three names from the oldest to youngest.

I have been reminded of your sincere faith, which first lived in your grandmother Lois and in your mother Eunice and, I am persuaded, now lives in you also.

1. _____
2. _____
3. _____

Note: Timothy's mother was a Jewish believer, but his father was Greek (Acts 16:1) and is thought to have been an unbeliever. That didn't keep Lois and Eunice from passing on their faith.

4. What do you think Lois and Eunice taught Timothy to help him develop a sincere faith? Read 2 Timothy 3:14, 15, and underline the basis of their teaching.

But as for you, continue in what you have learned and have become convinced of, because you know those from whom you learned it, and how from infancy you have known the holy Scriptures, which are able to make you wise for salvation through faith in Christ Jesus.

5. When was Timothy taught Scripture?

_____

_____

How did this benefit him?

_____

_____

6. As grandparents, what can we learn from Lois's example? List specific actions you can take to pass a sincere faith on to your grandchildren.

_____

_____

_____

_____

_____

These building blocks will help you transfer a lasting faith to your grandchildren:

Possess: First, you must possess a sincere faith. You can't give away something you don't have.

Purpose: You must purpose to intentionally pass on your faith. It won't happen by osmosis.

Portray: To pass on a sincere faith, set a godly example that demonstrates it.

Pray: Realize that sharing your faith requires praying for wisdom and guidance from the Holy Spirit.

Pass it on: Take time to share your faith when you're with your grandchildren or write to them. Pray they will understand salvation and accept Jesus.

7. Which of these building blocks do you need to focus on right now?

_____

_____

8. Paul tells Timothy how to set a good example for those he pastors. We can apply his teaching as grandparents. Read Paul's instructions to Timothy and underline the verbs:

Set an example for the believers in speech, in life, in love, in faith and in purity. (1 Timothy 4:12)

Watch your life and doctrine closely. Persevere in them, because if you do, you will save both yourself and your hearers. (1 Timothy 4:16)

Here's an example of one great-great-grandmother, now in her mid-eighties, who persevered throughout her life and reaped what 1 Timothy 4:16 says: salvation for her granddaughter.

Great-Great-Grandma Shirley's Story

"When my step-granddaughter came to visit me, we had a precious time together. Recently she had become a grandmother herself, and I listened as she shared the concerns on her heart. She asked many questions about God, Jesus, and the Bible, and I answered as simply as I could. Just before her departure, she said, 'I'm ready, Grandma.' I had prayed for this young woman throughout her life, so you can imagine my thrill when God used me to lead her to Jesus. After my granddaughter left, I wiped tears of joy from my eyes as I read her words in my guest book: 'This is the first day of a new life. You are a blessing to me. I love you.'"

Have you been praying a long time for God to work in someone's life, perhaps a child or grandchild? Take heart. Persevere. *"Watch your life and doctrine closely."* God is working, and He will reward you in His time.

Paul saw Timothy's sincere faith and potential. So he invested in Timothy's life and taught him spiritual truths. But Paul built on what Timothy had been taught from infancy by his grandmother, Lois, and mother, Eunice. He instructed Timothy, *"Guard the good deposit that was entrusted to you—guard it with the help of the Holy Spirit who lives in us"* (2 Timothy 1:14).

No one could take Lois's or Eunice's place in Timothy's life. Neither can anyone take your place as a grandparent. Others can add to your spiritual teaching, but they can't fill your God-given role.

As we pass along our faith, we can do so by sharing biblical truths and faith-building stories from our lives. We'll discuss faith stories later this week, so let's focus on specific truths from God's Word.

9. In Paul's writings to Timothy and Titus, he mentions several trustworthy sayings. They make a good place to begin sharing our faith. Read what Paul said, and then fill in what we could say to our grandchildren. The first one is completed as an example.

Paul said:	We could say:
Here is a trustworthy saying that deserves full acceptance: Christ Jesus came into the world to save sinners—of whom I am the worst. (1 Timothy 1:15)	Jesus died to save us because we are sinners.
This is a trustworthy saying that deserves full acceptance (and for this we labor and strive), that we have put our hope in the living God, who is the Savior of all men, and especially of those who believe. (1 Timothy 4:9, 10)	
Here is a trustworthy saying: If we died with him, we will also live with him; if we endure, we will also reign with him. (2 Timothy 2:11, 12)	
This is a trustworthy saying. And I want you to stress these things, so that those who have trusted in God may be careful to devote themselves to doing what is good. These things are excellent and profitable for everyone. (Titus 3:8)	

These verses emphasize that Jesus died for our sins and rose again from death. Certainly, that truth is the foundation of our faith. We long for our grandchildren to know and accept Jesus as Savior and Lord.

One of our pastors, Pastor Dean Osuch, demonstrated how to present the gospel in ten words. This might be a simple way to tell young grandchildren how to become Christians. And older grandchildren could use it to share the gospel with their friends. Start by holding up both hands. The right hand represents God and the left hand represents man. Repeat the words (in bold) aloud as you do the motions.

1. Both hands are clasped together.
God loves.

2. Left hand moves to the left.
We sinned.

3. Right hand moves to the right.
Jesus died.

4. Right hand moves to center.
God forgives.

5. Left hand moves to center; hands clasped.
We accept.

That's our desire—that our grandchildren accept Jesus and grow in their faith. The following examples tell how other grandparents pass on their faith:

Model: "Grandchildren watch what you say and do. They can see that church and Sunday school are important to us." Grandpa Bill

Share: "I often share what Jesus has done for me and the difference He's made in my life. I'm spontaneous in sharing His blessings." Grandma Donna

Write: "I'm writing my life story with an emphasis on my relationship with Jesus." Grandma Eva

Read: "Read Bible stories and let them know Jesus is a real person." Grandma Jeanne

Transport: "When our first grandson was two, our children weren't attending church regularly. We picked up our grandson and took him to Sunday school. Then he began asking his parents to take him, and they have." Grandma Carole

Teach: "We have devotions when the grandchildren are with us. Sometimes we gather around the piano and sing together." Grandma Sylvia

Apply to life: "We don't wait to talk about Jesus until we are praying or having a Bible lesson. We watch for everyday opportunities to bring the reality of Jesus into their lives." Grandma Shirley

Timothy received a rich heritage from his grandmother. What lasting legacy do you most desire to leave your grandchildren? Paul's charge to Timothy is one we can all embrace: *"Fight the good fight of the faith. Take hold of the eternal life to which you were called"* (1 Timothy 6:12).

With God's help, let's pass the baton of faith securely into the hands of future generations. Then we can say with Paul, *"I have fought the good fight, I have finished the race, I have kept the faith"* (2 Timothy 4:7).

GRAND Thought: No matter how rich or poor you are, you can give your grandchildren a tremendous gift—a legacy of faith. By providing a strong spiritual foundation, you'll influence not only the present generation but also all future generations, even after you're gone. Never underestimate the power of a grandparent's faith!

Prayer: Heavenly Father, thank You for showing us what a priceless inheritance looks like. Right now, You're keeping an inheritance for us in heaven that won't perish, spoil, or fade. And we want to lay up a rich heritage for our grandchildren. Help us stand firm in our faith and lay a strong foundation for them to build on. May they see that our faith in Jesus is real, and may they desire it for themselves. By Your Spirit, draw each grandchild to You. Just as You are faithful, Lord, help *us* to be faithful, unwavering, always abounding in Your work, knowing that our labor is not in vain. We accept the charge of Paul to Timothy to fight the good fight and to keep the faith.

(Based on 1 Peter 1:4; 1 Corinthians 15:58; 2 Timothy 4:7)

Love for God's Word

Day Two

As I tucked my eight- and ten-year-old grandsons into bed, I said, "I'll read to you from *The VeggieTales Bible* (a regular New International Version Bible with *VeggieTales* illustrations). They liked that idea, so I said, "I love the book of Joshua. Let's start at the first chapter."

"The Lord said to Joshua the son of Nun," I began, then joked, "Oh, I guess Joshua didn't have parents. He was the son of none!" Chapter 1 flew by as I asked them to count how

many times it said to be strong and courageous. When we finished, I said, "Chapter 2 is about spies."

"Ooooh, let's hear about the spies," said Alex.

So I continued. But as I read aloud about Rahab, I left out the word prostitute. I wasn't ready to explain it, and they weren't ready to hear it.

At the end of chapter 2, the heading "Crossing the Jordan" intrigued them, so I read chapters 3 and 4. At the end of chapter 4 I read, *"He did this so that all the peoples of the earth might know that the hand of the LORD is powerful and so that you might always fear the LORD your God"* (v. 24).

They were still interested, and I was about to continue until I noticed the heading for chapter 5 was "Circumcision at Gilgal."

"It's getting late, boys," I said. "Time to stop." Four chapters of the Old Testament had kept them engrossed, but I decided their parents could take on the concepts in chapter 5.

After I prayed with them, my grandson Peter's spontaneous prayer touched my heart and confirmed that the boys had indeed enjoyed God's Word. He prayed, "Thank you, God, for grandparents who like to have fun with us."

> *My grandmother was blind, so she never saw me. But when I visited, I sat on her lap, and we rocked and sang 'The Old Rugged Cross' and 'Amazing Grace.' I didn't attend church as a child, so this was my church. I learned Bible truths from these hymns. It was wonderful."*
> *Dianna*

Heartwork

Why Pass on a Love for God's Word?

In this lesson we'll discover why it's important to pass on a love for God's Word and how to do it.

1. As you read Psalm 19:7–11, list the names, truths (descriptions), and benefits of God's Word in the chart below.

> *The law of the LORD is perfect, reviving the soul. The statutes of the LORD are trustworthy, making wise the simple.*
>
> *The precepts of the LORD are right, giving joy to the heart. The commands of the LORD are radiant, giving light to the eyes.*

The fear of the LORD is pure, enduring forever. The ordinances of the LORD are sure and altogether righteous.

They are more precious than gold, than much pure gold; they are sweeter than honey, than honey from the comb.

By them is your servant warned; in keeping them there is great reward.

Names	Truths (descriptions)	Benefits
Law of the LORD	Perfect	Revives the soul

Speaking of sweeter than honey (v. 10), when our grandson turned ten, I mailed him an age-appropriate devotional and his favorite candy bars. I included this note:

Dear Peter,

Today we're sending you two sweet things: candy and God's Word. Which is sweeter? The Bible says God's Word is sweeter than honey from the honeycomb (Psalm 19:10). We pray you will always treasure God's Word. If you obey it, you'll be successful (Joshua 1:8).

The day you were born was a very happy day. We're glad God planned for you to be born into our family.

Love,

Grandpa and Grandma Tea

Inside the book of devotions, I wrote, "May God's Word be a lamp to your feet and a light to your pathway" (Psalm 119:105) and, *"I have hidden your word in my heart that I might not sin against you"* (Psalm 119:11).

My niece, Ann, encourages her children's understanding of the Word by having them draw pictures of verses. This is one way to pass on Scripture even before your grandchildren can form letters and words. Here is Ann's eleven-year-old daughter, Julia's, depiction of Psalm 119:11 and 105:

I have hidden your word in my heart that I might not sin against you. (Psalm 119:11)

Your word is a lamp to my feet and a light for my path. (Psalm 119:105)

Second Timothy 3:16, 17, offers four ways God's Word is profitable for us. *"All Scripture is God-breathed and is useful for teaching, rebuking, correcting and training in righteousness, so that the man of God may be thoroughly equipped for every good work."*

Here's how Ann's twelve-year-old daughter, Christine, illustrated God breathing these four benefits.

Sometimes a picture *is* worth a thousand words!

2. Because God's Word teaches, rebukes, corrects, and trains us, what are we then equipped to do?

_____

In 2 Timothy 3:17, note the words *thoroughly* (not *haphazardly*) and *every* (not *some*).

3. Hebrews 4:12 tells us what else God's Word can do. How might you draw a picture of this verse, or paraphrase it?

> *My granddaughter (age 21) asked if she could have my Bible after I die."*
> Grandma Eva

For the word of God is living and active. Sharper than any double-edged sword, it penetrates even to dividing soul and spirit, joints and marrow; it judges the thoughts and attitudes of the heart.

Psalm 119, with 176 verses, focuses on God's Word from beginning to end. This emphasis tells us how much God values His Word. Why not take fifteen minutes to read Psalm 119 aloud? Let it impact your life and increase your appreciation for God's Word. Your love for Scripture will encourage your grandchildren to have a love for the Bible.

How to Pass on a Love for God's Word

4. Look at the psalmist's view of God's Word in Psalm 119. How does he regard it? Read the verses and fill in the blanks.

Psalmist's Attitude toward God's Word

Verses from Psalm 119	Psalmist's View of God's Word
I rejoice in following your statutes as one rejoices in great riches (v. 14).	He _____ in it.
I delight in your decrees; I will not neglect your word (v. 16).	He _____ in it.
My soul is consumed with longing for your laws at all times (v. 20).	He _____ for it.
The law from your mouth is more precious to me than thousands of pieces of silver and gold (v. 72).	God's Word is _____ to him.
Oh, how I love your law! I meditate on it all day long (v. 97).	He _____ it and _____ on it.

Which of those attitudes express your view of God's Word? I continue to ask God for a greater love for His Word. If you want a growing love for the Bible, pray this prayer or one of your own:

Dear Lord, thank You that Your Word is true, powerful, and trustworthy. Give me a greater delight in it, so I don't neglect reading and obeying it. I know it's alive and powerful! Please give me a growing longing for Your laws, so I'll value them more than silver and gold. May I stand in awe of Your precious Word and rejoice in it.

5. I asked grandparents for specific ways to pass on a love for God's Word to their grandchildren. Here are some of their responses. Check those you'd like to try.

> *Grandma started her day at 5 a.m. by reading her Bible. That was the most important thing to her. As we got older, she would share her favorite verses with us." Lori*

- Let them see you reading the Bible.
- Read Bible stories to them from an early age. If available, use the same books you used to read to your kids.
- Tell Bible stories in exciting ways; consider acting them out together.
- Use Bible characters and events as illustrations when you explain things about life.
- Sing Bible songs and hymns, such as "Jesus Loves Me" and "Amazing Grace."
- Answer their questions about the Bible.
- Apply Bible lessons to their lives in relevant ways.
- Give age-appropriate Bibles as gifts.
- Memorize God's Word yourself, encourage them to memorize it, and memorize it together.
- Send letters, and include relevant Bible verses.
- As you travel, talk about God's Word.
- Encourage them to have a regular devotional time.
- Play Bible Trivia and other games that teach them about the Bible.
- Take them to Sunday school to learn about Jesus and His Word.

> *We read the children's Bible together, and they see me reading my Bible. Recently when I had my Bible open, my grandson said, 'You read that every day, don't you?' He sees my living faith—that's important." Grandma Bonnie*

The night I read from Joshua to my grandsons at bedtime, I realized that passing along a love for God's Word is like passing on treasure, because God's Word leads to prosperity and success. Joshua 1:8 says:

> *Do not let this Book of the Law depart from your mouth; meditate on it day and night, so that you may be careful to do everything written in it.* ***Then you will be prosperous and successful.*** [emphasis added]

Even if I'm not wealthy, I can leave my grandchildren a rich heritage. If I help them know and obey God's Word, they will be prosperous and successful. What a joy to know that when we share God's Word with our grandchildren, we're passing on the truth and helping them walk in truth!

> Heaven and earth will pass away, but my words will never pass away. (Mark 13:31)

GRAND Thought: God's Word will last forever. So when we pass on a love for God's Word to our grandchildren, we give them an eternal treasure.

Prayer:

May my lips overflow with praise, for you teach me your decrees.
May my tongue sing of your word, for all your commands are righteous.
May your hand be ready to help me, for I have chosen your precepts.
I long for your salvation, O LORD, and your law is my delight.
Let me live that I may praise you, and may your laws sustain me.

(Psalm 119:171–175)

Lord, Your Word is powerful. Give me a deep, abiding love for Your teaching and truth.

Day Three

Excitement for Prayer

More than thirty relatives crowded into my niece's home for our bimonthly prayer time. We had gathered to celebrate a total of fifty years of cancer remission among several family members.

The adults sat in the living room, and the children, ranging in age from three to seventeen, lined the stairway going up from there. We began by singing praises to God. The children requested their favorite choruses, and we also sang hymns, such as "Great Is Thy Faithfulness." As I recalled God's faithfulness to me, one of the cancer survivors, tears rolled down my cheeks. I wasn't the only one with misty eyes.

We also thanked God for answered prayers. Our short prayers, one after another, were like popcorn popping as three generations voiced their thanksgiving. The children prayed simple, sincere prayers from the heart, such as: "Thank you for my brother and sister."

Then we split into groups to pray for requests gathered beforehand.

As the evening ended, we sensed it had been a holy time. A grandmother said, "It was pretty awesome to hear all the grandkids pray, and see they felt at ease and knew what to pray about."

Family members parted with hugs and smiles, and I knew God was smiling, too.

Heartwork

Perhaps you're saying, "My family would never get together to pray," or, "We don't have a large Christian family."

1. According to Jesus' teaching, how many does it take to have an effective prayer time? Read Matthew 18:19, 20, and underline how many need to gather for God to be present:

> *Again, I tell you that if two of you on earth agree about anything you ask for, it will be done for you by my Father in heaven. For where two or three come together in my name, there am I with them.*

What does God promise if two or more gather to pray? Do you know one other believer who would meet with you to pray for your family? If so, God promises to join you.

But prayer times don't just happen. Although I come from a Christian family, we weren't in the habit of praying together as an extended family. God convicted my husband and me to start family prayer times, and we purposed to begin, whether others joined us or not. We already had the required quota of two. Thankfully, others wanted to pray, and over the past twelve years, many have joined us.

To pass on a legacy of prayer, these three things are important: (1) Make prayer a **priority,** (2) believe in the **power and promises** of prayer, and (3) **persevere** in prayer. We'll look briefly at each.

Make Prayer a Priority

We need to be *intentional* about passing on an excitement for prayer. Realize from the start that it won't happen without a struggle. You'll have a tug of war between God and Satan. God wants to empower you to persevere in prayer, and the devil wants to discourage you and set up roadblocks. But 1 John 4:4 assures us who wins the battle: *"The one who is in you is greater than the one who is in the world."*

Even as I write this, schedule conflicts make it hard for many to attend our next family prayer time, so we'll have a smaller group. But it doesn't take a crowd for God to join us, hear our prayers, and answer according to His will.

Jesus modeled prayer. He prayed in solitude, at night, before performing miracles, or before making big decisions.

2. Read the following verses that show how Jesus made prayer a priority. What can we learn from His example as we pray for our grandchildren and give them a legacy of prayer?

> *Jesus went out to a mountainside to pray, and spent the night praying to God. When morning came, he called his disciples to him and chose twelve of them, whom he also designated apostles.* (Luke 6:12, 13)

_____

_____

> *Very early in the morning, while it was still dark, Jesus got up, left the house and went off to a solitary place, where he prayed.* (Mark 1:35)

But Jesus often withdrew to lonely places and prayed.
(Luke 5:16)

_____

_____

These verses are only a sampling of the times Jesus prayed.

What would motivate you to give your grandchildren (or anyone else) an excitement for prayer? Jesus' priority for prayer encourages me to model prayer. But I'm also motivated to pray because God hears and answers prayer. Prayer is powerful! As a friend said, "This prayer thing does work."

Believe in the Power and Promises of Prayer

Do you ever question whether God works through prayer? Have you waited a long time for an answer and wondered if it would ever come? I have. The Bible contains many examples of how God answered prayer, and some individuals (like Hannah in week 3 and Simeon and Anna in week 5) also waited a long time. The Bible includes promises that assure us God *does* hear and answer. Let's claim these promises and share them with our grandchildren.

3. Read the following verses about prayer, and list the promises found in them. Some verses include conditions to receive answers. Write those conditions in the third column.

Prayer Promises

Verses	Promises	Conditions
Before they call I will answer; while they are still speaking I will hear. (Isaiah 65:24)		
If you believe, you will receive whatever you ask for in prayer. (Matthew 21:22)		
If any of you lacks wisdom, he should ask God, who gives generously to all without finding fault, and it will be given to him. But when he asks, he must believe and not doubt. (James 1:5, 6)		

The prayer of a righteous man is powerful and effective. (James 5:16)		
Dear friends, if our hearts do not condemn us, we have confidence before God and receive from him anything we ask, because we obey his commands and do what pleases him. (1 John 3:21, 22)		
This is the confidence we have in approaching God: that if we ask anything according to his will, he hears us. And if we know that he hears us—whatever we ask—we know that we have what we asked of him. (1 John 5:14, 15)		

Do these promises reinforce your desire to pray? As you read your Bible, add more promises to the chart.

4. Remembering past answers to prayer encourages me to continue praying. Can you recall recent answers to prayer for your grandchildren? If so, write them below. If the answer relates to one of the prayer promises in the chart, place a check by the verse. Share answers to prayer with others.

Share your enthusiasm for prayer by telling your grandkids about answers to prayer. Also, ask them how you can pray for them, and ask them to pray for you.

_____

_____

_____

_____

Persevere in Prayer

Jesus taught His disciples how to pray in the Lord's Prayer, and he also taught them principles of prayer through parables.

Let's consider the parable in Luke 18:1–8.

5. Although the meaning of a parable usually comes at the end, Luke 18:1 begins by telling the disciples the point of the parable. Underline the six-word formula that says when we should pray and for how long.

> *¹Then Jesus told his disciples a parable to show them that they should always pray and not give up. ²He said: "In a certain town there was a judge who neither feared God nor cared about men. ³And there was a widow in that town who kept coming to him with the plea, 'Grant me justice against my adversary.' ⁴"For some time he refused. But finally he said to himself, 'Even though I don't fear God or care about men, ⁵yet because this widow keeps bothering me, I will see that she gets justice, so that she won't eventually wear me out with her coming!'"*

Always pray? To apply Luke 18:1, we can pray *first*—before making decisions—and continue praying about ongoing concerns.

6. Let's look at the two main characters in the parable and compare them. Fill in the traits for the judge and the widow in the chart below:

Judge's Character Traits   **Widow's Character Traits**

What do we know about the judge from these verses? (See verses 2, 4, and 5.)	What do we learn about the widow from these verses? (See verses 3 and 5.)

The judge possessed status and authority, and he had the power to grant the widow's request. The widow was weak in political power, probably poor, and without an advocate to help her. With which person do you identify?

Now read the rest of the parable and look for the contrast between the judge and Jesus:

> [6]And the Lord said, "Listen to what the unjust judge says. [7]And will not God bring about justice for his chosen ones, who cry out to him day and night? Will he keep putting them off? [8]I tell you, he will see that they get justice, and quickly." Luke 18:6–8

_____

_____

7. What can we learn about God and prayer from Luke 18:1–8?

_____

_____

_____

How does verse 7 reinforce what verse 1 tells us concerning when to pray and how long to pray?

_____

This parable not only shows that God answers, it also tells us He wants us to keep asking. How have you viewed repeated prayers? As pestering God, or persisting?

As we continually bring our requests to God, we aren't nagging to wear Him down. No, instead we come like the widow—powerless and needy—knowing God is eager to answer prayer for our good and for His glory. And as we wait for His timing and spend time in prayer, our relationship with Him deepens. If God doesn't answer immediately, we can be confident that, from His eternal viewpoint, there's a reason. As we persevere in prayer, we combine faith and patience and place our hope in God. And while we wait, God is working. So the bottom line is: Never give up![10]

Years ago I wrote a poem that emphasized the need to persevere in prayer during every season of life:

A Lifetime of Prayer

As a young mother,
I bowed in prayer,
"Lord, keep my children
In your tender care."

A young grade school mother,
More fervent my prayers,
"Protect my dear children;
Remove all my cares."

A junior high mother,
Intent on my knees,
"Lord, keep them from evil,"
More anxious my pleas.

A college-age mother,
Empty nest now in view,
"Lord, guide all their choices;
Draw them closer to you."

A mother still faithful,
How soothing to pray
For my grown children,
"Lord, teach *them* to pray."

A gray-haired grandmother
Well-seasoned in prayer,
With confidence upholding
Generations in prayer.

A mother in heaven
One day I'll be,
Praising my Savior
Who heard every plea.

8. We've studied three aspects of prayer: Make prayer a **priority**, believe in the **power and promises** of prayer, and

persevere in prayer. All three will help us give others an excitement for prayer. Which one stands out as most important for you now? Ask God to help you grow in one or more of these areas. Record your prayer here:

_____

_____

_____

_____

GRAND Thought: As grandparents, we need to model prayer. If we're excited about praying, those who see and hear us pray will be excited, too. God wants to help us give our grandchildren a strong legacy of prayer.

Prayer: Loving Father, I praise You that You keep all Your promises. I can count on Your Word that says You hear and answer prayer. Although I know Your Word is true, sometimes my faith wavers. I confess I become impatient waiting for answers and want to quit praying. And sometimes I lose hope and even doubt that You will answer. Please forgive me. Strengthen my faith and my resolve to pray. Encourage me through Your Word and Your answers. I trust Your timing and commit to pray consistently and persistently. You are my God, and I want my grandchildren to see I love You and love to pray. Ignite my passion for prayer, and help my family and me to always pray and not give up.

Day Four

Faith Stories

When Katie's fifth-grade class was assigned to give oral heritage reports, Katie gathered information about her German great-grandparents, Nicolai and Helena Siemens. She also asked her Grandma Ruth to bake zwieback (a yeast double bun) to serve her classmates. During her report, Katie told how her great-grandpa was imprisoned for being a Christian and was almost sent to Siberia. But instead he was released from the Russian prison. Then she shared this story: "When my great-grandpa was on a train in Russia and didn't have any money, a stranger sat beside him, gave him a handful of money, and then disappeared. Grandpa thought the man was an angel!"

When Katie finished, one girl asked, "Do you think it was an angel?"

"Yes," Katie said with conviction.

As I write this story, tears run down my cheeks because Katie's great-grandfather was my father. Without his release from the Moscow prison and God's provision, my grandchildren and I would not have been born.

Heartwork

As we tell the next generation about the great things God has done, their faith in God will grow, and they'll better understand their heritage. Plus, they can share these stories with others.

Do our children and grandchildren know our faith stories? Are we telling our stories or recording them? Psalm 102:18 says, *"Let this be written for a future generation, that a people not yet created may praise the LORD."*

1. God's Word mentions specific things we can tell others. Read the verses in the following chart, and list what we're told to pass on. The first is filled in as an example.

Bible verses	What should we share with our families?
Even when I am old and gray, do not forsake me, O God, till I declare your power to the next generation, your might to all who are to come. (Psalm 71:18)	God's power and might
Then we your people, the sheep of your pasture, will praise you forever; from generation to generation we will recount your praise. (Psalm 79:13)	
One generation will commend your works to another; they will tell of your mighty acts. (Psalm 145:4)	
We will not hide them from their children; we will tell the next generation the praiseworthy deeds of the LORD, his power, and the wonders he has done. (Psalm 78:4)	

Psalm 78:7 records the outcome of telling future generations the Lord's deeds and laws: *"Then they would put their trust in God and would not forget his deeds and would keep his commands."*

2. What mighty acts and praiseworthy deeds has God done for your family? List them, and plan ways to share them face-to-face, in writing, or by recording them (tape, CD, DVD).

_____

_____

_____

My son's family has a shadow box hanging on their wall that reminds them of God's praiseworthy deeds. The small objects inside represent times when God intervened and cared for them in special ways. For example, a wooden heart with a hole in it reminds them their toddler survived open-heart surgery.

> I will remember the deeds of the LORD; yes, I will remember your miracles of long ago.
> (Psalm 77:11)

The Bible not only encourages us to remember and pass on what God has done. It also encourages us to set up stones of remembrance. Let's look at two biblical examples.

3. Read 1 Samuel 7:3–13 to learn how God delivered the children of Israel from the Philistines. Note what they did to commemorate His deliverance. I've highlighted the parts that stood out to me. Underline words and phrases that impact you.

> And Samuel said to the whole house of Israel, *"If you are **returning to the LORD with all your hearts**, then **rid** yourselves of the foreign gods and the Ashtoreths and **commit** yourselves to the LORD and **serve him only**, and he will **deliver** you out of the hand of the Philistines."*
>
> *So the Israelites **put away** their Baals and Ashtoreths, and **served the LORD only**.*
>
> *Then Samuel said, "Assemble all Israel at Mizpah and **I will intercede** with the LORD for you."*
>
> *When they had assembled at Mizpah, they drew water and poured it out before the LORD. On that day they **fasted** and there they **confessed**, "We have sinned*

against the LORD." And Samuel was leader of Israel at Mizpah.

When the Philistines heard that Israel had assembled at Mizpah, the rulers of the Philistines came up to attack them. And when the Israelites heard of it, they were afraid because of the Philistines.

*They said to Samuel, **"Do not stop crying out to the LORD our God for us,** that he may rescue us from the hand of the Philistines."*

*Then Samuel took a suckling lamb and **offered it** up as a whole burnt offering **to the LORD**. He cried out to the LORD on Israel's behalf, and the LORD answered him.*

*While Samuel was sacrificing the burnt offering, **the Philistines drew near** to engage Israel in battle. But that day **the LORD thundered** with loud thunder **against the Philistines** and threw them into such a panic that **they were routed** before the Israelites.*

The men of Israel rushed out of Mizpah and pursued the Philistines, slaughtering them along the way to a point below Beth Car.

Then Samuel took a stone and set it up between Mizpah and Shen. He named it Ebenezer, saying, "Thus far has the LORD helped us."

*So the Philistines were subdued and did not invade Israelite territory again. **Throughout Samuel's lifetime, the hand of the LORD was against the Philistines.***

Ebenezer means "stone of help."

4. Why would this be a good story to pass on, especially if the next generation hadn't witnessed the victory? What spiritual truths or lessons does it teach?

_____

_____

_____

5. Why do you think Samuel set up a memorial stone between Mizpah and Shen? How would that help the Israelites tell this story?

_____

_____

Years ago, after my husband read this passage, he suggested we make an Ebenezer to commemorate the fact that *"Thus far the LORD has helped us"* in our marriage. So Milt and I gathered sixteen small stones at the beach, one for each year of marriage, and a smooth, fifteen-inch piece of driftwood. Once home, we glued the stones onto the driftwood and set a parchment sign beside it that said "Our Ebenezer" and the words from 1 Samuel 7:12. My husband isn't particularly sentimental, so it was special that he suggested this. Our children found security in seeing this simple witness of God's faithfulness. As we approach our forty-third anniversary, our Ebenezer not only reminds us God has helped us this far, but that He'll continue to help us.

God's Word includes other times when memorial stones were erected to remember God's faithfulness. For example, when God parted the Jordan River and the Israelites passed through on dry ground, God instructed Joshua to appoint one Israelite from each tribe to do as follows:

> *"Go over before the ark of the LORD your God into the middle of the Jordan. Each of you is to take up a stone on his shoulder, according to the number of the tribes of the Israelites, to serve as a sign among you. In the future, when your children ask you, 'What do these stones mean?' tell them that the flow of the Jordan was cut off before the ark of the covenant of the LORD. When it crossed the Jordan, the waters of the Jordan were cut off. These stones are to be a memorial to the people of Israel forever."*
> (Joshua 4:5–7)

6. What are the Ebenezers in your life? What memorial stones can you share with your family?

_____

_____

_____

_____

Your stories may not seem as dramatic as these biblical examples, but they're important.

- Did God sustain you through a serious illness? Tell your grandchildren that as Jehovah-Rapha, God heals.

- Did He provide a job during economically hard times? Tell your loved ones Jehovah Jireh provides.
- Did someone encourage you or pray for you when you needed courage?
- Did God answer a specific prayer?
- Did God comfort you during a loss? Tell others that because of Jehovah Shalom, God's peace surrounds you.
- Is there a special verse God used to build your faith or to help you through a hard time?

These are all part of your life story and would bless your grandchildren. Faith-building stories are part of your spiritual heritage and the legacy you can pass on to future generations. But passing them on won't *just happen*. It takes planning and follow-through.

When my father was in his eighties, he recorded highlights from his life and self-published them in a book. He literally fulfilled Psalm 102:18: *"Let this be written for a future generation, that a people not yet created may praise the LORD."* As a result, his unborn great-grandchildren, such as Katie, can share stories of God's faithfulness and bring praise to God.

GRAND Thought: God wrote your life story, and it has meaning for you and your grandchildren. He has a purpose for each scene and chapter. As we share stories of God's work in our lives, we pass on a rich spiritual heritage, and these stories help build our grandchildren's faith.

> Remember the days of old; consider the generations long past. Ask your father and he will tell you, your elders, and they will explain to you. (Deuteronomy 32:7)

Prayer: Heavenly Father, our eternal, unchanging God, we thank You for the rich heritage we have through Christ Jesus. Thank You that, through Jesus' death for our sins and the power of His resurrection, we can become Your children. It's both unthinkable and glorious that You welcome me, a sinful pauper, into a relationship with You, the King of kings and Lord of lords. I want to pass along this marvelous story of Your salvation and forgiveness to future generations. But I also want to share other praiseworthy deeds and mighty acts You have performed for my family and me. Help me see Your fingerprints in my daily life, and show me how to tell my family and others what great things You have done.

Day Five — Generational Blessings

We've run twenty-nine laps around the grandparenting Bible study track, and this is our last one. It's been a marathon, not a sprint. You are dedicated grandparents, and you've stayed the course. Today we'll study how God blesses our obedience and how we can leave a legacy of blessings for our grandchildren. Let's continue, and finish strong!

> But you, O LORD, sit enthroned forever; your renown endures through all generations.
> (Psalm 102:12)

Heartwork

Years ago, two Bible verses stood out to me in sharp contrast. They shaped my focus in parenting and grandparenting.

1. Read the following verses, and note the far-reaching blessing for obedience and the sobering consequences for disobedience.

> *¹And God spoke all these words: . . . ³"You shall have no other gods before me. . . .*
> *⁵You shall not bow down to them or worship them; for I, the LORD your God, am a jealous God, punishing the children for the sin of the fathers to the third and fourth generation of those who hate me, ⁶but showing love to a thousand [generations] of those who love me and keep my commandments.* (Exodus 20:1, 3, 5, 6)

2. Based on these verses, fill in the chart. The "obedience" column is already completed.

Consequences of Obedience and Disobedience

	Disobedience (verse 5)	Obedience (verse 6)
Behavior listed		Love God and keep His commandments
Consequences		Experience God's love
Length of time		A thousand generations

Deuteronomy 7:9 also speaks of blessings for obedience: *"Know therefore that the LORD your God is God; he is the faithful God, keeping his covenant of love to a thousand generations of those who love him and keep his commands."*

These verses influenced my priorities because I realized my obedience would impact future generations for good. The converse was too frightening to consider. I wanted my descendants to reap blessings.

Nonetheless, my husband and I aren't perfect. Early in our marriage God showed us issues to deal with. Together we knelt by our bed, confessed sins, and asked God to break specific generational sin patterns we did not want passed on.

> *Although my parents never met their great-grandchildren (my grandchildren), their godly heritage continues and reaches the third and fourth generations." Grandma Ruth*

No doubt you want to leave a godly legacy, too. And you *can*—even if you have generational sins in your family of origin, and even if you're the only person in your family who loves God. *You* can be the transitional person who starts a lineage of obedience and reaps blessings for future generations. If you need help to break a destructive cycle, I encourage you to pray and seek assistance. Talk to your pastor or a godly counselor. God wants to free you and your descendants and bring blessings, not punishment. He has the power to bring about change and victory. God can restore *"years the locust has eaten"* (Joel 2:25). God can *"do exceeding abundantly above all that we ask or think"* (Ephesians 3:20 KJV).

We may come from a long line of God-fearing ancestors, or we may be the first generation in our family to embrace

Jesus as *"the way and the truth and the life"* (John 14:6). However, like Esther in the Bible, God has placed us here as grandparents *"for such a time as this"* (Esther 4:14). We can make a difference in the lives of generations yet unborn. We can pass on blessings to our descendants.

3. The chart below lists verses that show how we can bless our offspring by following God. List the blessings, and the conditions to receive them. The first is completed as an example.

Verses	Blessings	Conditions
But from everlasting to everlasting the LORD's love is with those who fear him, and his righteousness with their children's children—with those who keep his covenant and remember to obey his precepts. (Psalm 103:17, 18)	The Lord's love God's righteousness	Fear Him Keep His covenant and obey His precepts
He holds victory in store for the upright, he is a shield to those whose walk is blameless, for he guards the course of the just and protects the way of his faithful ones. (Proverbs 2:7, 8)		
For the LORD God is a sun and shield; the LORD bestows favor and honor; no good thing does he withhold from those whose walk is blameless. (Psalm 84:11)		
Blessed is the man who fears the LORD, who finds great delight in his commands. His children will be mighty in the land; the generation of the upright will be blessed. (Psalm 112:1, 2)		
His mercy extends to those who fear him, from generation to generation. (Luke 1:50)		

Aren't these hope-filled verses? Our godly lives can result in our grandchildren following God and receiving His love, righteousness, favor, honor, mercy, victory, protection, and all other good things, *and* they will be mighty! Isn't that what we want for them?

> **The righteous man leads a blameless life; blessed are his children after him.**
> **(Proverbs 20:7)**

4. Read these additional verses that promise blessing. Then write a prayer asking God to bless your grandchildren.

For I will pour water on the thirsty land, and streams on the dry ground; I will pour out my Spirit on your offspring, and my blessing on your descendants. (Isaiah 44:3)

Now be pleased to bless the house of your servant, that it may continue forever in your sight; for you, O Sovereign LORD, have spoken, and with your blessing the house of your servant will be blessed forever. (2 Samuel 7:29)

Blessings crown the head of the righteous. (Proverbs 10:6)

The blessing of the LORD brings wealth, and he adds no trouble to it. (Proverbs 10:22)

The memory of the righteous will be a blessing. (Proverbs 10:7)

Lord, I pray these blessings for my grandchildren:

_____

_____

_____

_____

Besides passing on generational blessings by our obedience, we can also bless our grandchildren with well-chosen words. The Bible includes numerous examples of fathers and grandfathers blessing their offspring in a ceremony, and two are even listed in Hebrews 11, the great hall of faith:

> *I can be one of my grandchildren's best memories. I will die in their lifetime. I want to leave them with a positive picture of God."*
> *Grandma Debbie*

By faith Isaac blessed Jacob and Esau in regard to their future.

By faith Jacob, when he was dying, blessed each of Joseph's sons, and worshiped as he leaned on the top of his staff. (Hebrews 11:20, 21)

The rest of the story of how Jacob blesses his grandsons Ephraim and Manasseh is found in Genesis 48. Jacob is near death and Joseph brings his sons to see their grandfather. Jacob, now called Israel, says to Joseph, *"Bring them to me so I may bless them"* (v. 9). Then Jacob adds, *"I never expected to see your face again, and now God has allowed me to see your children too"* (v. 11). Can't you sense Israel's profound joy in seeing his grandsons, and hear the emotion in his words?

After Israel kissed and embraced his grandsons, he placed his hands on their heads and blessed them.

5. Read his blessing from Genesis 48:15, 16. What can we learn from Israel's blessing of his grandsons?

"May the God before whom my fathers Abraham and Isaac walked, the God who has been my shepherd all my life to this day, the Angel who has delivered me from all harm—may he bless these boys. May they be called by my name and the names of my fathers Abraham and Isaac, and may they increase greatly upon the earth."

_____

_____

_____

Remember that Hebrews 11:21 says, *"He worshiped as he leaned on the top of his staff."* In much of Jacob's blessing he praises God. I felt touched that Israel's blessing of his grandsons centered on worshipping God. After all, it was God he was asking to bless them. By himself, he couldn't make them increase, deliver them from harm, or cause them to follow the God of his fathers.

Giving a blessing is not only an Old Testament custom. God Himself blessed His Son. After Jesus' baptism, a voice from heaven said, *"This is my Son, whom I love; with him I am well pleased"* (Matthew 3:17).

Would you like to give a spoken or written blessing to your grandchildren? If so, here are some components of a blessing. You'll find more on the subject of blessing others in Gary Smalley's and John Trent's book *The Blessing*.[11] On the Web, www.christiangrandparenting.net offers tips and examples. (Click on main resource bar.)

To bless your grandchildren:

- Picture a bright future for them. Tell them what they do well. Let them know you believe in them and that you have confidence they will succeed in God's purposes for them.
- Tell them they are special and that you love them. Words like "Good job" and "I'm proud of you" and "I'm happy to be your grandparent" will encourage them. Besides words, show your love as Grandpa Israel did in Genesis 48:10 (embraced and kissed his grandsons).
- Tell them you highly value them. Choose a characteristic, look them in the eye, and express how you appreciate that trait in them. Beyond words, reinforce their value by making time for them in your life.
- With your words and actions, help them reach the blessing you have given them.

Your blessing could be given at a special occasion, such as a birthday, graduation, or spiritual milestone. But don't just wait for special occasions. Speak words of affirmation whenever you're with your grandchildren or write to them.

6. Ephesians 4:29 guides us in how to speak to our grandchildren:

> *Do not let any unwholesome talk come out of your mouths, but only what is helpful for building others up according to their needs, that it may benefit those who listen.*

List the dos and don'ts.

Do _____

Don't _____

Also, your grandchildren will feel blessed when you give them:

- acceptance
- affection
- approval
- appreciation
- attention

7. Jot ideas to pass on a written or spoken blessing to one or more grandchildren.

_____

_____

_____

_____

Then one day a grandchild may bless you in return. Tyler did this when he wrote a graduation letter to his grandparents, who helped his single mother raise him. Here's an excerpt:

"The two of you mean more to me than I can explain. The relationship you have with each other is what I dream of with my future wife. The stability and foundation you have in your faith in God is something I long for. And when I grow up, I want to be like you. With all the love in the world, Tyler-Dean"

Grandma Joyce shared, "When we read Tyler's letter, it was like the Lord saying to us that all those years of loving him and being there for him and our daughter were blessed by God and were worth every minute of time and effort."

We all long for affirmation and blessing not only from our earthly family but also from God the Father. As we continue to run the race with perseverance, in order to win the prize (Hebrews 12:1 and 1 Corinthians 9:24), one day we'll hear our heavenly Father say, *"Well done, good and faithful servant!"* (Matthew 25:23).

So keep running. You're a winner! Everything you invest in your grandchildren will be worth it. Although you can't see it now, the blessings you'll receive in the future will be

> **Do you not know that in a race all the runners run, but only one gets the prize? Run in such a way as to get the prize.**
> **(1 Corinthians 9:24)**

far greater than the time and effort you've invested into your grandchildren.

GRAND Thought: As you live a godly, obedient life, the generational blessings you leave for your present and future grandchildren are beyond anything you can imagine!

Prayer: Thank You, Lord, that You are a shelter for every generation. And because You never change, Your faithfulness continues to all generations. As we run our race on Earth and pass the baton of faith into the hands of the next generation, help us finish strong. We trust You with our lives and the lives of our grandchildren.

As we conclude this final lesson, I pray this blessing for you:

> *The LORD bless you and keep you;*
> *the LORD make his face shine upon you and be gracious to you;*
> *the LORD turn his face toward you and give you peace.*
> *May the LORD make you increase, both you and your children.*
> *May you be blessed by the LORD, the Maker of heaven and earth.*

(Numbers 6:24–26; Psalm 115:14, 15)

Weekend Devotion

Passing the Baton of Faith

Future generations will be told about the Lord. They will proclaim his righteousness to a people yet unborn. (Psalm 22:30, 31)

Read: Psalm 22:25–31

Our four-day family reunion was coming to a close. Three generations, ranging in age from one month to seventy-two years, were gathered to strengthen family bonds and share God's faithfulness. We recalled many exciting stories, such as our father's miraculous release from a Russian prison during the same hour his brother's church in America prayed for his deliverance. As we shared our lives, we saw evidence of

God's love and blessings all around us, including the twelve preschool children born into our families. Two of them were our grandsons.

As we concluded the reunion, I anticipated the final reunion in heaven, and prayed that not one in our family would be missing. Then we formed a large circle and passed a "baton of faith" from hand to hand. As we did so, each person said, "I will be faithful to Jesus and follow in His footsteps." Slowly the baton circled the group. It came full circle when my niece's son passed it to me, repeating, "I will be faithful to Jesus and follow in His footsteps." Our eyes clouded as we hugged.

As a Christian family, it is our deep desire to tell future generations about the Lord and to proclaim God's righteousness to generations yet unborn. Family reunions are one way we intentionally share our faith.

A few months after the reunion, my niece's twenty-year-old son e-mailed me saying, "I found my faith again at the family reunion." Later, he was baptized and led a Bible study on his college campus. We have no greater joy than to know that our family members walk in God's truth.

Prayer: Righteous God of our fathers, we remember Your goodness to us and thank You for Your blessings. We bow down and acknowledge You as the Ruler over all the families of the nations. May our families today and in all future generations worship You alone.

Appendix

Path to Salvation

These verses will help you begin a new relationship with God. They explain how to invite Him to become the loving Leader in your life.

1. God loves.

"For God so loved the world that he gave his one and only Son, that whoever believes in him shall not perish but have eternal life" (John 3:16).

God loves you and created you for a purpose. He wants to have a personal relationship with you.

2. We sinned.

"For all have sinned and fall short of the glory of God" (Romans 3:23).

Because of our sins (disobeying God and going our own way), we are separated from a holy (sinless) God.

3. Jesus died.

"But God demonstrates his own love for us in this: While we were still sinners, Christ died for us" (Romans 5:8).

God had a plan to bring us back to Him. He sent His Son to die to save us from our sins.

4. God forgives.

"If we confess our sins, he is faithful and just and will forgive us our sins and purify us from all unrighteousness" (1 John 1:9).

If we turn from our sins and ask for forgiveness, God will forgive us.

5. We accept.

"Yet to all who received him, to those who believed in his name, he gave the right to become children of God" (John 1:12).

Once we accept God's free gift of salvation, which comes through Jesus, we become part of God's family.

If you want to turn your life over to God, pray a prayer something like this:

Dear God, I know I'm a sinner. Thank You for sending Jesus to die for me. Please forgive my sins. I want to turn from my wrongdoings and receive Jesus as my Savior. Thank You for forgiving me. I give You control of my life and want to follow You. In Jesus' name. Amen.

If you prayed this prayer as an act of faith, then 2 Corinthians 5:17 is true of you: *"Therefore, if anyone is in Christ, he is a new creation; the old has gone, the new has come!"*

To grow in Christ:
1. Tell someone of your new faith in Christ.
2. Find and attend a church that solidly teaches the Word of God.
3. Talk to God in prayer every day, and read the Bible—His love letter to you.

You can receive a free weekly devotional at billygraham.org/decision. If you have questions or need help to grow in your faith, e-mail: help@bgea.org, or call 1-877-247-2426.

Suggestions for Leaders

Invite a group of "expectant" grandparents and those with years of experience and wisdom for a time of fellowship and study. The beauty of varied ages and stages means those with more experience in grandparenting can share what they have learned and thus apply the biblical principle of the older teaching the younger (Titus 2:3–5). Those new in the role may bring insights the others haven't considered.

Grandparenting is an exciting, challenging role. Ask God to bless and inspire the grandparents in your group so they catch the vision and joy of grandparenting. My desire is that this study will help readers pass on a godly heritage to their grandchildren.

Although *Preparing My Heart for Grandparenting* is written as a six-week study, the lessons can be divided so it becomes a twelve-week (or longer) study—for groups who want more discussion time. If you prefer to meet for six weeks, ask group members to come with specific questions they would like to discuss.

On Your Mark . . . Plan to meet for one-and-a-half to two hours. For the first meeting, encourage grandparents to bring photos of their grandchildren to share to help everyone become acquainted. Most grandparents are eager to bring their brag books.

Get Set . . . I suggest you begin and end your meeting with prayer. If group members feel comfortable praying aloud, you could plan time at the end to share requests and pray together. You could also share requests and then pray for each other's grandchildren during the week.

If your group shows interest, schedule an extra meeting time to pray for the grandchildren. Week 2 includes a prayer format you could follow. For groups of six or more, consider splitting into twos or threes to allow time to pray for all the grandchildren.

Grow! . . . Encourage group members to apply the lessons in personal, practical ways. But no one needs to be a "super-grandparent" and try to do everything suggested. Let God's Spirit direct group members on what to apply. This study isn't meant to make anyone feel guilty for what they have or haven't done. Instead, let it become a springboard to move forward and grow as grandparents.

Thank you for your commitment to future generations. You're making an eternal impact. Investing in grandchildren is worth the time and effort. And it's fun, too! I commend you for passing on a legacy of faith. God bless you.

Now may the God of peace who brought up our Lord Jesus from the dead, that great Shepherd of the sheep, . . . make you complete in every good work to do His will . . . through Jesus Christ, to whom be glory forever and ever. Amen. (Hebrews 13:20, 21, NKJV).

Resources

Grandparenting

1. Bly, Stephen, and Janet Bly. *The Power of a Godly Grandparent.* Kansas City, MO: Beacon Hill Press, 2003.
2. Campbell, D. Ross, M.D., with Rob Suggs. *How to Really Love Your Grandchild.* Ventura, CA: Regal, 2008.
3. Coleman, Bill, and Pat Coleman. *Every Thursday: A Warm, Loving Look at Grandparenting.* Grand Rapids, MI: Discovery House Publishers, 2004. (Devotional book)
4. Hosier, Helen Kooiman. *Living the Lois Legacy: Passing on a Lasting Faith to Your Grandchildren.* Wheaton, IL: Tyndale House Publishers, 2002.

Prayer

1. Dean, Jennifer Kennedy. *Legacy of Prayer: A Spiritual Trust Fund for the Generations.* Birmingham, AL: New Hope Publishers, 2002.
2. Sherrer, Quin, and Ruthanne Garlock. *Grandma, I Need Your Prayers: Blessing Your Grandchildren through the Power of Prayer.* Grand Rapids, MI: Zondervan, 2002.
3. Wayne, Melanie K. *A Grandparent's Prayer Journal: Lifting My Grandchildren to the Throne of Grace.* Mustang, OK: Tate Publishing, LLC, 2006.

For Grandchildren

1. Christenson, Evelyn, and Liz Duckworth. *What Happens When Children Pray: Learning to Talk and Listen to God.* Colorado Springs: David C. Cook, 2005.

2. Omartian, Stormie. *What Happens When I Talk to God?* Eugene, OR: Harvest Hous Publishers, 2007.

3. Taylor, Jeannie St. John. *Am I Praying?* Grand Rapids, MI: Kregel KidZone, 2003.

4. *The Truth Chronicles: Adventures in Odyssey.* Based on the Truth Project. Colorado Springs: Focus on the Family, 2009. (Compact disc, ages 8–12)

Bibles and Bible Studies

1. *The Grandmother's Bible.* New International Version. Grand Rapids, MI: Zondervan, 2008. (Includes prayers to pray for grandchildren and devotions for grandmothers)

2. Other Bible studies in the "Preparing My Heart" series:
   Preparing My Heart for Advent
   Preparing My Heart for Easter
   Preparing My Heart for Motherhood

Endnotes

1. *NIV Encouragement Bible,* New International Version, Joni Eareckson Tada and Dave and Jan Dravecky, (Grand Rapids, Michigan: Zondervan Publishing House, 2001), 1087.

2. Based on an article, "Why Don't People Pray?" by Jon Detweiler, Northshore Baptist Church, Bothell, Washington.

3. Ibid.

4. *NIV Encouragement Bible,* 346.

5. Based on a message by Pastor Jan David Hettinga, Northshore Baptist Church, Bothell, Washington, 1994.

6. Meyer, Joyce, *Secrets to Exceptional Living* (Tulsa, OK: Harrison House, 2002), 14.

7. *NIV Encouragement Bible,* 1464.

8. Ibid., 1582.

9. Ibid., 1582.

10. Background insights for Luke 18 came from: Gary Inrig, *The Parables: Understanding What Jesus Meant* (Grand Rapids, MI: Discovery House Publishers, 1991) 149–159.

11. Gary Smalley and John Trent, *The Blessing* (Nashville, TN: Thomas Nelson, 1986).